# Perimeter Defense Mechanisms

## EC-Council I Press

Volume 3 of 5 mapping to

# E |NSA™

EC-Council | Network Security
Administrator

Certification

**COURSE TECHNOLOGY**
CENGAGE Learning™

Australia • Brazil • Japan • Korea • Mexico • Singapore • Spain • United Kingdom • United States

# COURSE TECHNOLOGY
## CENGAGE Learning™

**Perimeter Defense Mechanisms**
**EC-Council | Press**

Course Technology/Cengage Learning
   Staff:

Vice President, Career and Professional
   Editorial: Dave Garza

Director of Learning Solutions:
   Matthew Kane

Executive Editor: Stephen Helba

Managing Editor: Marah Bellegarde

Editorial Assistant: Meghan Orvis

Vice President, Career and Professional
   Marketing: Jennifer Ann Baker

Marketing Director: Deborah Yarnell

Marketing Manager: Erin Coffin

Marketing Coordinator: Shanna Gibbs

Production Director: Carolyn Miller

Production Manager: Andrew Crouth

Content Project Manager:
   Brooke Greenhouse

Senior Art Director: Jack Pendleton

**EC-Council:**

President | EC-Council: Sanjay Bavisi

Sr. Director US | EC-Council:
   Steven Graham

For product information and technology assistance, contact us at
**Cengage Learning Customer & Sales Support, 1-800-354-9706**

For permission to use material from this text or product,
submit all requests online at **www.cengage.com/permissions**.
Further permissions questions can be e-mailed to
**permissionrequest@cengage.com**

Library of Congress Control Number: 2010924350

ISBN-13: 978-1-4354-8357-6

ISBN-10: 1-4354-8357-X

**Cengage Learning**
5 Maxwell Drive
Clifton Park, NY 12065-2919
USA

Cengage Learning is a leading provider of customized learning solutions with office locations around the globe, including Singapore, the United Kingdom, Australia, Mexico, Brazil, and Japan. Locate your local office at: **international.cengage.com/region**

Cengage Learning products are represented in Canada by
Nelson Education, Ltd.

For more learning solutions, please visit our corporate website at **www.cengage.com**

Printed in the United States of America
1 2 3 4 5 6 7   13 12 11 10

# Table of Contents

## CHAPTER 4
## Bastion Hosts and Honeypots . . . . . . . . . . . . . . . . . . . . . . . . . . . . . . . . . . . . . . . . . . . . . . . . . . . **4-1**

## CHAPTER 5
## Wireless Network Security . . . . . . . . . . . . . . . . . . . . . . . . . . . . . . . . . . . . . . . . . . . . . . . . . . . . . . **5-1**

Hacking and electronic crimes sophistication has grown at an exponential rate in recent years. In fact, recent reports have indicated that cyber crime already surpasses the illegal drug trade! Unethical hackers better known as *black hats* are preying on information systems of government, corporate, public, and private networks and are constantly testing the security mechanisms of these organizations to the limit with the sole aim of exploiting it and profiting from the exercise. High profile crimes have proven that the traditional approach to computer security is simply not sufficient, even with the strongest perimeter, properly configured defense mechanisms like firewalls, intrusion detection, and prevention systems, strong end-to-end encryption standards, and anti-virus software. Hackers have proven their dedication and ability to systematically penetrate networks all over the world. In some cases *black hats* may be able to execute attacks so flawlessly that they can compromise a system, steal everything of value, and completely erase their tracks in less than 20 minutes!

The EC-Council Press is dedicated to stopping hackers in their tracks.

# About EC-Council

The International Council of Electronic Commerce Consultants, better known as EC-Council was founded in late 2001 to address the need for well-educated and certified information security and e-business practitioners. EC-Council is a global, member-based organization comprised of industry and subject matter experts all working together to set the standards and raise the bar in information security certification and education.

EC-Council first developed the *Certified Ethical Hacker,* C|EH program. The goal of this program is to teach the methodologies, tools, and techniques used by hackers. Leveraging the collective knowledge from hundreds of subject matter experts, the C|EH program has rapidly gained popularity around the globe and is now delivered in over 70 countries by over 450 authorized training centers. Over 80,000 information security practitioners have been trained.

C|EH is the benchmark for many government entities and major corporations around the world. Shortly after C|EH was launched, EC-Council developed the *Certified Security Analyst,* E|CSA. The goal of the E|CSA program is to teach groundbreaking analysis methods that must be applied while conducting advanced penetration testing. E|CSA leads to the *Licensed Penetration Tester,* L|PT status. The *Computer Hacking Forensic Investigator,* C|HFI was formed with the same design methodologies above and has become a global standard in certification for computer forensics. EC-Council through its impervious network of professionals, and huge industry following has developed various other programs in information security and e-business. EC-Council Certifications are viewed as the essential certifications needed where standard configuration and security policy courses fall short. Providing a true, hands-on, tactical approach to security, individuals armed with the knowledge disseminated by EC-Council programs are securing networks around the world and beating the hackers at their own game.

# About the EC-Council | Press

The EC-Council | Press was formed in late 2008 as a result of a cutting edge partnership between global information security certification leader, EC-Council and leading global academic publisher, Cengage Learning. This partnership marks a revolution in academic textbooks and courses of study in Information Security, Computer Forensics, Disaster Recovery, and End-User Security. By identifying the essential topics and content of EC-Council professional certification programs, and repurposing this world class content to fit academic programs, the EC-Council | Press was formed. The academic community is now able to incorporate this powerful cutting edge content into new and existing Information Security programs. By closing the gap between academic study and professional certification, students and instructors are able to leverage the power of rigorous academic focus and high demand industry certification. The EC-Council | Press is set to revolutionize global information security programs and ultimately create a new breed of practitioners capable of combating the growing epidemic of cybercrime and the rising threat of cyber-war.

# Network Defense Series

The EC-Council | Press *Network Defense* series, preparing learners for E|NSA certification, is intended for those studying to become secure system administrators, network security administrators and anyone who is interested in network security technologies. This series is designed to educate learners, from a vendor neutral standpoint, how to defend the networks they manage. This series covers the fundamental skills in evaluating internal and external threats to network security, design, and how to enforce network level security policies, and ultimately protect an organization's information. Covering a broad range of topics from secure network fundamentals, protocols & analysis, standards and policy, hardening infrastructure, to configuring IPS, IDS and firewalls, bastion host and honeypots, among many other topics, learners completing this series will have a full understanding of defensive measures taken to secure their organizations information. The series when used in its entirety helps prepare readers to take and succeed on the E|N|SA, Network Security Administrator certification exam from EC-Council.

Books in Series
- *Network Defense: Fundamentals and Protocols*/1435483553
- *Network Defense: Security Policy and Threats*/1435483561
- *Network Defense: Perimeter Defense Mechanisms*/143548357X
- *Network Defense: Securing and Troubleshooting Network Operating Systems*/1435483588
- *Network Defense: Security and Vulnerability Assessment*/1435483596

## Perimeter Defense Mechanisms

*Perimeter Defense Mechanisms* discusses the importance of enhancing the security of physical assets, how firewalls can be used to bolster network security, an introduction to packet filtering and proxy servers, bastion hosts and honeypots, and the basics of wireless networks and their security.

# Chapter Contents

Chapter 1, *Hardening Physical Security*, includes coverage of the need for and ways to enhance physical security. Chapter 2, *Firewalls*, discusses many aspects of this network gateway server including security features, threats and security risks and logs and tools. Chapter 3, *Packet Filtering and Proxy Servers*, includes the basics and different types of packet filtering and the role of proxy servers. Chapter 4, *Bastion Hosts and Honeypots,* covers the basics of bastion, or hardened, hosts and honeypots and teaches how to deploy and configure them. Chapter 5, *Wireless Network Security*, discusses the concepts of wireless networks and how to secure them.

# Chapter Features

Many features are included in each chapter and all are designed to enhance the learner's learning experience. Features include:

- *Objectives* begin each chapter and focus the learner on the most important concepts in the chapter.
- *Key Terms* are designed to familiarize the learner with terms that will be used within the chapter.
- *Chapter Summary*, at the end of each chapter, serves as a review of the key concepts covered in the chapter.
- *Review Questions* allow the learner to test their comprehension of the chapter content.
- *Hands-On Projects* encourage the learner to apply the knowledge they have gained after finishing the chapter. Files for the *Hands-On Projects* can be found on the Student Resource Center. Note: you will need your access code provided in your book to enter the site. Visit *www.cengage.com/community/eccouncil* for a link to the Student Resource Center.

# Student Resource Center

The Student Resource Center contains all the files you need to complete the Hands-On Projects found at the end of the chapters. Access the Student Resource Center with the access code provided in your book. Visit *www.cengage.com/community/eccouncil* for a link to the Student Resource Center.

# Additional Instructor Resources

Free to all instructors who adopt the *Perimeter Defense Mechanisms* book for their courses is a complete package of instructor resources. These resources are available from the Course Technology web site, *www.cengage.com/coursetechnology*, by going to the product page for this book in the online catalog, and choosing "Instructor Downloads".

Resources include:

- *Instructor Manual*: This manual includes course objectives and additional information to help your instruction.
- *ExamView Testbank*: This Windows-based testing software helps instructors design and administer tests and pre-tests. In addition to generating tests that can be printed and administered, this full-featured program has an online testing component that allows students to take tests at the computer and have their exams automatically graded.
- *PowerPoint Presentations*: This book comes with a set of Microsoft PowerPoint slides for each chapter. These slides are meant to be used as a teaching aid for classroom presentations, to be made available to students for chapter review, or to be printed for classroom distribution. Instructors are also at liberty to add their own slides.
- *Labs*: Additional Hands-on Activities to provide additional practice for your students.
- *Assessment Activities*: Additional assessment opportunities including discussion questions, writing assignments, internet research activities, and homework assignments along with a final cumulative project.
- *Final Exam*: Provides a comprehensive assessment of *Perimeter Defense Mechanisms* content.

# Cengage Learning Information Security Community Site

This site was created for learners and instructors to find out about the latest in information security news and technology.

Visit *community.cengage.com/infosec* to:

- Learn what's new in information security through live news feeds, videos and podcasts.
- Connect with your peers and security experts through blogs and forums.
- Browse our online catalog.

# How to Become E|NSA Certified

The E|NSA certification ensures that the learner has the fundamental skills needed to analyze the internal and external security threats against a network, and to develop security policies that will protect an organization's information. E|NSA certified individuals will know how to evaluate network and Internet security issues and design, and how to implement successful security policies and firewall strategies as well as how to expose system and network vulnerabilities and defend against them.

E|NSA Certification exams are available through Prometric Prime. To finalize your certification after your training, you must:

1. Purchase an exam voucher from the EC-Council Community Site at Cengage: *www.cengage.com/community/eccouncil*.
2. Speak with your Instructor or Professor about scheduling an exam session, or visit the EC-Council Community Site referenced above for more information.
3. Take and pass the E|NSA certification examination with a score of 70% or better.

# About Our Other EC-Council | Press Products

## Ethical Hacking and Countermeasures Series

The EC-Council | Press *Ethical Hacking and Countermeasures* series is intended for those studying to become security officers, auditors, security professionals, site administrators, and anyone who is concerned about or responsible for the integrity of the network infrastructure. The series includes a broad base of topics in offensive network security, ethical hacking, as well as network defense and countermeasures. The content of this series is designed to immerse the learner into an interactive environment where they will be shown how to scan, test, hack and secure information systems. A wide variety of tools, viruses, and malware is presented in these books, providing a complete understanding of the tactics and tools used by hackers. By gaining a thorough understanding of how hackers operate, ethical hackers are able to set up strong countermeasures and defensive systems to protect their organization's critical infrastructure and information. The series when used in its entirety helps prepare readers to take and succeed on the C|EH certification exam from EC-Council.

Books in Series
- *Ethical Hacking and Countermeasures: Attack Phases*/143548360X
- *Ethical Hacking and Countermeasures: Threats and Defense Mechanisms*/1435483618
- *Ethical Hacking and Countermeasures: Web Applications and Data Servers*/1435483626
- *Ethical Hacking and Countermeasures: Linux, Macintosh and Mobile Systems*/1435483642
- *Ethical Hacking and Countermeasures: Secure Network Infrastructures*/1435483650

## Computer Forensics Series

The EC-Council | Press *Computer Forensics* series, preparing learners for C|HFI certification, is intended for those studying to become police investigators and other law enforcement personnel, defense and military personnel, e-business security professionals, systems administrators, legal professionals, banking, insurance and other professionals, government agencies, and IT managers The content of this program is designed to expose the learner to the process of detecting attacks and collecting evidence in a forensically sound manner with the intent to report crime and prevent future attacks. Advanced techniques in computer investigation and analysis with interest in generating potential legal evidence are included. In full, this series prepares the learner to identify evidence in computer related crime and abuse cases as well as track the intrusive hacker's path through client system.

Books in Series
- *Computer Forensics: Investigation Procedures and Response*/1435483499
- *Computer Forensics: Investigating Hard Disks, File and Operating Systems*/1435483502
- *Computer Forensics: Investigating Data and Image Files*/1435483510
- *Computer Forensics: Investigating Network Intrusions and Cybercrime*/1435483529
- *Computer Forensics: Investigating Wireless Networks and Devices*/1435483537

## Penetration Testing Series

The EC-Council | Press *Penetration Testing* series, preparing learners for E|CSA/LPT certification, is intended for those studying to become Network Server Administrators, Firewall Administrators, Security Testers, System Administrators and Risk Assessment professionals. This series covers a broad base of topics in advanced penetration testing and security analysis. The content of this program is designed to expose the learner to groundbreaking methodologies in conducting thorough security analysis, as well as advanced penetration testing techniques. Armed with the knowledge from the Penetration Testing series, learners will be able to perform the intensive assessments required to effectively identify and mitigate risks to the security of the organization's infrastructure. The series when used in its entirety helps prepare readers to take and succeed on the E|CSA, Certified Security Analyst certification exam.

E|CSA certification is a relevant milestone towards achieving EC-Council's Licensed Penetration Tester (LPT) designation, which also ingrains the learner in the business aspect of penetration testing. To learn more about this designation please visit *http://www.eccouncil.org/lpt.htm*.

Books in Series
- *Penetration Testing: Security Analysis*/1435483669
- *Penetration Testing: Procedures and Methodologies*/1435483677
- *Penetration Testing: Network and Perimeter Testing*/1435483685
- *Penetration Testing: Communication Media Testing*/1435483693
- *Penetration Testing: Network Threat Testing*/1435483707

## Cyber Safety/1435483715

*Cyber Safety* is designed for anyone who is interested in learning computer networking and security basics. This product provides information cyber crime; security procedures; how to recognize security threats and attacks, incident response, and how to secure internet access. This book gives individuals the basic security literacy skills to begin high-end IT programs. The book also prepares readers to take and succeed on the Security|5 certification exam from EC-Council.

## Wireless Safety/1435483766

*Wireless Safety* introduces the learner to the basics of wireless technologies and its practical adaptation. *Wireless|5* is tailored to cater to any individual's desire to learn more about wireless technology. It requires no pre-requisite knowledge and aims to educate the learner in simple applications of these technologies. Topics include wireless signal propagation, IEEE and ETSI Wireless Standards, WLANs and Operation, Wireless Protocols and Communication Languages, Wireless Devices, and Wireless Security Network. The book also prepares readers to take and succeed on the Wireless|5 certification exam from EC-Council.

## Network Safety/1435483774

*Network Safety* provides the basic core knowledge on how infrastructure enables a working environment. Intended for those in an office environment and for the home user who wants to optimize resource utilization, share infrastructure and make the best of technology and the convenience it offers. Topics include foundations of networks, networking components, wireless networks, basic hardware components, the networking environment and connectivity as well as troubleshooting. The book also prepares readers to take and succeed on the Network|5 certification exam from EC-Council.

## Disaster Recovery Series

The *Disaster Recovery Series* is designed to fortify virtualization technology knowledge of system administrators, systems engineers, enterprise system architects, and any IT professional who is concerned about the integrity of the their network infrastructure. Virtualization technology gives the advantage of additional flexibility as well as cost savings while deploying a disaster recovery solution. The series when used in its entirety helps prepare readers to take and succeed on the E|CDR and E|CVT, Disaster Recovery and Virtualization Technology certification exam from EC-Council. The EC-Council Certified Disaster Recovery and Virtualization Technology professional will have a better understanding of how to setup Disaster Recovery Plans using traditional and virtual technologies to ensure business continuity in the event of a disaster.

Books in Series
- *Disaster Recovery*/1435488709
- *Virtualization Security*/1435488695

# Acknowledgements

Michael H. Goldner is the Chair of the School of Information Technology for ITT Technical Institute in Norfolk Virginia, and also teaches bachelor level courses in computer network and information security systems. Michael has served on and chaired ITT Educational Services Inc. National Curriculum Committee on Information Security. He received his Juris Doctorate from Stetson University College of Law, his undergraduate degree from Miami University and has been working over fifteen years in the area of Information Technology. He is an active member of the American Bar Association, and has served on that organization's Cyber Law committee. He is a member of IEEE, ACM and ISSA, and is the holder of a number of industrially recognized certifications including, CISSP, CEH, CHFI, CEI, MCT, MCSE/Security, Security +, Network + and A+. Michael recently completed the design and creation of a computer forensic program for ITT Technical Institute, and has worked closely with both EC-Council and Delmar/Cengage Learning in the creation of this EC-Council Press series.

# Chapter 1

# Hardening Physical Security

## Objectives

**After completing this chapter, you should be able to:**

- Understand the need for physical security
- Understand the factors that affect network security
- Recognize specific physical security threats
- Implement premises security
- Apply biometrics in physical security
- Implement workplace security
- Secure network devices
- Understand the challenges in ensuring physical security
- Implement physical security measures
- Develop a physical security checklist

## Key Terms

**Faraday cage**   a metallic enclosure or cage that prevents the entry or escape of an electromagnetic field by having a fine-mesh copper screening embedded into the walls or system container

**Script kiddies**   unskilled hackers who generally use downloaded applications to break into systems

## Introduction to Hardening Physical Security

In addition to securing the network from external software attacks, the physical security of assets must be ensured. The following parts of the network must be physically secure:

- Servers
- Workstations
- Devices that enable access to the network, such as routers, switches, bridges, and hubs
- Network wiring

- Access points
- Laptops
- IT financial assets and credentials

This chapter will familiarize you with physical security as well as the steps that need to be taken in order to increase that security.

# Understanding the Need for Physical Security

There are many different physical attack threats to a network; however, most fall into one of the following three categories, based on the specific way in which the attack occurs:

1. Forced entry threats
2. Ballistic threats
3. Explosive blast threats

Each of the three categories covers specific types of attacks, such as sabotage and burglary. In many cases security can be completely compromised if physical access is achieved. Attackers can disable, reconfigure, replace, and/or steal systems with relative ease once physical security is breached.

## Statistics

- According to the CSI/FBI Computer Crime Security Survey 2005, nearly 40% of victims fail to report computer intrusions.
- According to Nationwide Mutual Insurance, 16% of debit card attack victims bear the total cost, or a part of the cost, of fraudulent purchases up to $4,000.
- According to Nationwide Mutual Insurance, one-third of consumers report their online banking IDs becoming compromised. Hackers gained 21% of this compromised bank account information through the victims' homes, cars, mailboxes, trash, wallets, or other physical means.
- The Global State of Information Security 2005 survey revealed that 37% of those surveyed had an information security strategy and that 24% of respondents are still developing a process for securing their bank account information.

## Internet Security

The network manager will follow different network policies depending upon whether the network is trusted, untrusted, or unknown.

### *Trusted Networks*

Trusted networks are inside the network security perimeter, so every computer in the network is behind a common firewall. This also includes VPNs. Firewalls are arranged to specify the location where the network packets originated so a server can authenticate the location.

### *Untrusted Networks*

These are external networks outside the security perimeter. They are not under the complete control of the network administrator or the security policies.

### *Unknown Networks*

Unknown networks are networks that are neither trusted nor untrusted, because the firewall is not aware of them.

## Physical Security Breach Incidents

Any breach of security is a serious concern. Physical security breaches are a serious offense under the law and there have been many incidents of people being prosecuted for such breaches, including the following:

- In 2001, Yasuo Takei, chairman of Japan's biggest consumer lender, Takefuji, was arrested on charges of wiretapping. Metropolitan Police Department investigators suspected Takei of ordering former Takefuji official Kazuhiro Nakagawa to wiretap a journalist and others to protect his son. In addition, Naka-gawa confessed to police that he had also wiretapped the communications of a former branch head of the company.

- In 2003, a laptop containing the names, addresses, and Social Security numbers of approximately 43,000 customers was stolen from the principal data-processing provider of Bank Rhode Island, Fiserv.
- On December 15, 2003, Jesus C. Diaz, who once worked as an AS/400 programmer for Hellmann Worldwide Logistics, was sentenced to a one-year imprisonment for accessing the company's computer system remotely and deleting critical OS/400 applications. Diaz caused more than $80,000 in damage. As a result of his actions, Hellmann Worldwide Logistics' AS/400 systems were down for 48 hours.

## Who Is Accountable for Physical Security?

Each employee is responsible for the systems that he or she handles. To strengthen the physical security of a company, the following personnel should be made accountable for physical and information security:

- The physical location's security officer
  - Responsible for any physical security breach
  - Responsible for educating the rest of the employees and guards on duty
  - Responsible for manually checking the firm's physical security periodically
- Safety officer
  - Responsible for fire protection
  - Responsible for educating employees and other staff on safety
- Information systems analyst or security administrator
  - Looks into network security and related issues
- Chief information officer
  - Heads the committee that frames security policies

# Understanding the Factors That Affect Network Security

## Vandalism

Disgruntled or former employees may try to compromise the system. Also, in any case where a disaster causes panic, systems may be mishandled.

## Theft

Lack of proper security may result in equipment theft. A guard on the premises can help prevent this.

## Natural Factors

### Earthquakes

Even minor earthquakes may cause dust and debris to fall on computer equipment. Plastic sheets should be readily available in the system room. Covering computing assets in an emergency may mitigate damage. Magnetic tapes should be covered to prevent wear and tear. Operators should be trained on how to properly cover the equipment.

### Fire and Smoke

Fire alarms and extinguishers should be placed well within the reach of employees, and they should be checked regularly to ensure proper functioning. Smoke detectors should be placed throughout the building. The desig-nated smoking area should be as far as possible from computer systems.

### Flood

Periodic inspections under the floors must be conducted to check for water seepage, especially during times of heavy precipitation. Water detectors must also be checked periodically. Administrators should be aware of proper shutdown procedures, and exercise drills must be performed regularly.

### Lightning and Thunder

All computer systems should have a UPS (uninterruptible power supply) so that voltage fluctuations, sudden power surges, and outages will not affect them. These incidents can cause significant damage to computer hardware, particularly the memory.

### Dust

Dust that naturally accumulates on hardware hinders its performance. Dust can seriously hinder a PC's ability to cool down. Even if the computer's case has never been opened, dust can still get in through the drive openings. An effective way to remove dust from the inside of a CPU is with compressed air, which can be used to blow dust away from the motherboard and other components.

### Water

PCs should not be placed near water sources or near windows. PCs should be placed in an environment where humidity is controlled.

### Explosion

Chemicals should be isolated and kept away from computers.

## Types of Attackers

While attackers differ in their intentions and procedures, their common aim is to identify technical flaws in security policies and take advantage of them.

### The Explorer

Purely out of curiosity, the explorer exploits security vulnerabilities and ends up breaking security policies. He or she browses through all sites, simply exploring and trying to figure out how things work. He or she tries to crack passwords, as well as alter or delete file settings and network configurations, but does not have any intention to cause real harm.

### The Discontented Worker

Ex-employees and current, dissatisfied employees can attempt to harm the company's resources. They can effectively attack the integrity, privacy, and accessibility of assets. Because they are familiar with the weaknesses of the security policies and the location of confidential information, they try to damage and dismantle assets with knowledge of the best places to attack.

### The Spy

Spies could be from intelligence agencies that attempt to obtain critical and confidential information. They could also be from rival companies, committing crimes for financial gain and reputation.

### The Terrorist

Terrorists use the Internet to carry out their plans. Terrorists might use information that isn't critical to a company and is less secured.

### The Thief

Thieves' primary concern is monetary gain. They try to acquire credit card information and reroute money offshore. They will often use social engineering to accomplish their goals.

### The Hacktivist

Hacktivists protest governments and try to destroy public assets. Examples of hacktivist activities include:

- DDoS attacks
- Web page defacements of government sites
- Antiglobalization protests

### The Script Kiddies

Unskilled hackers known as *script kiddies* use downloaded scripts and other automated attack tools to break into sites. They are often ignorant of what happens when they have access to sites and assets. Some hackers hire these script kiddies to perform DDoS attacks and to compromise the computers on a network.

### Hacker for Hire

There are two types of hackers for hire:

- The sneaker, also known as an ethical hacker, attempts to determine vulnerabilities and alert the owners of those vulnerabilities before any damage can be done.
- Mercenary hackers exploit the vulnerabilities of a company's Web site and sell the information to the highest bidder.

### The Competition

Competition between companies can lead to corporate espionage, in which one company spies on another or sabotages its computer systems.

### Enemy Countries

Rival countries regularly attack each others' information security.

## Physical Security Threats to Networks

Threat is defined as any event that can cause damage to an asset. The purpose of physical security is to ensure the confidentiality, integrity, and availability of assets, including the safety of all personnel.

Physical security is perhaps the most overlooked aspect of security. Generally, threats to physical security are categorized into the following types:

- Natural/environmental
- Human-made
- Supply system
- Political events

### Natural/Environmental

This type of threat includes the results of naturally occurring events, including:

- Flood
- Fire
- Earthquakes

### Flood

Floods commonly occur due to heavy rains or the melting of ice. This increases the level of water beyond the carrying capacity of a nearby river, resulting in a flood. Some types of floods increase slowly, taking days to pose a threat. On the other hand, flash floods come quickly without any sign of rain. In addition to water, this can cause rocks and mud to enter the area.

Earthquakes, mass movements above or below water, volcanic eruptions and other underwater explosions, landslides, large meteorite impacts, and weapons testing at sea all have the potential to generate a tsunami.

*Preventive Measures* The following preventive measures can help guard against flood damage on a global scale (though carefully choosing the site location is often the best solution):

- Constructing flood control dams
- Building dikes and levees beside rivers to prevent them from overflowing
- Building canals to leave room for extra water
- Regulating flood plain development and urbanization

- Preventing soil from eroding
- Planting many trees, treating slopes, and building reservoirs to catch sediment and debris
- Diverting rivers and streams away from populated areas

### Fire

Computers can be secured against fire threats by ensuring that there is good fire extinguishing equipment nearby and that personnel are trained to use it. A full sprinkler system should be installed in the building. The wiring should be protected, in addition to the computers. The organization should install smoke detectors and sprinkler heads that are appropriately positioned to cover wires and wiring closets.

### Earthquakes

Personnel should pay careful attention to the location of shelves and bookcases. They should avoid placing computers on high surfaces or near windows and avoid placing heavy objects on shelves near computers where they may fall onto the equipment. Computers should be placed on strong tables. Also, those involved in physical security concerns should consider physically attaching computers to surfaces.

## Human-Made Threats

The biggest threat to the physical components of an organization and its network are from human-made errors, be they intentional or unintentional. Human error includes hitting the wrong button, unplugging the wrong cord, and so on.

### Terrorism

Terrorist activities include the following:

- Assassinations
- Bombings
- Random killings
- Hijackings

### War

Wars destroy the major buildings, industries, and infrastructures of a particular country. Pollution can spread due to bombs and expelled gases. War also changes the economic conditions of many countries.

### Dumpster Diving

Dumpster diving involves searching the garbage of the targeted company in order to acquire important information. Attackers search for information such as phone numbers, credit card numbers, and other information commonly thrown away. Discarded storage media such as floppy disks, CDs, and tapes can also be used to obtain important information.

To prevent losses from dumpster diving, an organization should consider these countermeasures:

- Create a well-defined policy to handle important security-related information. This policy states how to deal with sensitive information, including how to store, delete, and edit the information. All employees must be trained in this policy.
- A strong magnet can be used to completely delete the data on magnetic storage devices, such as floppy disks, tapes, and hard drives.
- Documents containing confidential information must be shredded when they are no longer needed. Dumpsters should be locked and well lit to ensure that no unauthorized person tries to access them.
- Secure network configuration files from unauthorized access by keeping track of equipment information.
- Avoid sticking notes on monitors, routers, and network devices. Notes containing router information and locations of systems and devices provide an easy map to an attacker.
- Printouts of user logs must be shredded.
- All systems should be password protected.

### *Political Events*

Bombings, strikes, terrorism, riots, espionage, wars, and so on can affect the security of an organization and its normal operations. This falls under the basic need to avoid allowing physical access by any unauthorized persons.

## Detecting Physical Hazards

A safety program always starts with hazard detection, which involves the deliberate search and identification of unsafe conditions in a work place. This requires a good knowledge of acceptable standards, codes, regulations, and safe work practices.

Hazard detection involves the following:

- Physical inspection
- Accident investigation
- Accident analysis

### *Physical Inspection*

A physical inspection can be formal or informal. Regular inspections help personnel detect unsafe conditions.

### *Accident Investigation*

Once an accident occurs, it must be investigated based on all facts, statements, opinions, and related information. This includes recommending corrective actions to prevent the accident from reoccurring.

### *Accident Analysis*

An accident analysis is a collection of data taken from different accident information. If an accident is reported and investigated, the information from the investigation is included in this analysis to detect unsafe conditions and hazards.

### *Workplace Security*

Employees manage and store the confidential information on desktops, laptops, and portable storage devices for both their office and home facilities. Facility managers must be equipped to determine who has entered the premises, as well as what information they have accessed. These managers should use technologies such as smart cards, encryption keys, digital signatures, and biometrics in preventing unauthorized access.

# Implementing Premises Security

The premises are the physical area where computer hardware is located. The premises range from a limited space to a complete building. The location of the computers has to be decided after considering various conditions and security issues. The amount of hardware being used determines the space needed for the equipment. The cost and sensitivity of the devices are also considered when deciding on the location of the hardware.

## Security Considerations

- When necessary services are unavailable, the flow of business operations is negatively affected.
- Sudden damages to physical assets endanger business functions.
- Unauthorized access to systems leads to theft and damage of resources.
- Fire, floods, and failure of air conditioners can lead to damage of physical resources.
- Unauthorized visitors can access and corrupt unsecured information.

## Office Security

Some unsecured places where office information can be found are workstations, work areas, dustbins, and monitors. If an attacker can access such work areas in an office, he or she can gain information about passwords, user accounts, physical devices, and other security features. Locations vulnerable to displaying secure information include the following:

- Employees might fix sticky notes with password or account details to the computer monitor.
- Employees might leave sensitive information in desks, drawers, display boards, notebooks, and recycle bins next to printers, phones, or fax machines.
- Attackers may easily guess the system ID from the user ID and password.
- If an attacker gains access to a notebook with a list of passwords or user IDs, he or she can often guess the rest.
- If the list of telephone numbers is available to the hacker, he or she can gain information through social engineering.
- If the attacker knows the security policies adopted by the organization, he or she can more easily hide applications from the organization's security tools.
- From memos, the attacker can obtain network configurations, services, access privileges, etc.
- The attacker can obtain the internal manuals of the organization that explain the operations of different departments, which can show the hacker potential vulnerabilities.
- The attacker can determine the best time to attack if the calendar of events is accessible.

### Reception Area

In the reception area, outsiders entering the company must be observed. If they are strangers, their behavior should be recorded. Their intensions have to be noted. Extra attention should be paid to the following:

- Solicitors
- Charity organizations
- Ex-employees
- Movers

## Smart Cards

A smart card is a credit card–sized plastic device that contains a computer chip and memory. It can store, process, and output data securely. Smart cards commonly store cryptographic keys, digital certificates, identification credentials, and other information. They provide strong two-factor authentication using a PIN.

The International Organization for Standardization (ISO) uses the term *integrated circuit card* (ICC) instead of *smart card*.

### Benefits of Smart Cards

There are many benefits of smart cards, including the following:

- Lower administrative costs
- Reduced losses and liabilities
- Increased convenience
- Provides additional functionality, such as credential storage
- Provides strong two-factor authentication, with the possibility of a third, by using a fingerprint reader on the smart card itself
- Uses public-key cryptography without storing the key on a computer
- Can store multiple passwords
- Can be used anywhere inside or outside the building

### Smart Card Uses

One of the important factors behind smart card use is the fact that multiple applications are involved in the use of a smart card. A smart card provides portable secure storage for digital certificates. The smart card can also be used for many applications, such as the following:

- Logon/logoff authentication to an operating system
- Authentication to a Web site

- Sending/receiving e-mail
- Encryption of data files

## Types of Smart Cards

There are three types of smart cards:

- Stored-value cards
- Cryptographic coprocessor cards
- Optical-memory cards

*Stored-Value Cards (SVCs)* The stored-value card is the most common and least expensive of the smart cards. It stores data much like a magstripe card.

*Cryptographic Coprocessor Cards* Cryptographic coprocessor cards, or crypto cards, have specialized processors on board with specific support for cryptographic operations, such as digital signing and encryption.

*Optical-Memory Cards* An optical-memory card is a plastic card that stores information using lasers. These cards look somewhat like a credit card with a piece of a CD-ROM glued on top of the card. Because information is actually burned into the material during the write cycle, the medium is a write-once read-many (WORM) medium, and the data are nonvolatile (not lost when power is removed).

## Smart Card Components

Every manufacturer of smart cards has its own international design and proprietary systems. Nearly all smart cards have the same components. These common components include a CPU, memory, and an interface pad. The CPU is the brain of the smart card, much like the CPU of a PC. It contains the interface pads that provide access to the smart card. The smart card memory is in different forms based on the design. It uses random access memory (RAM), read-only memory (ROM), and electrically erasable programmable read-only memory (EEPROM), which is read and write capable.

## Contact and Contactless Cards

Contact cards have an electric contact on the card, while contactless cards use wireless technology to communicate. The distance covered by a contactless card can range from a few inches to a few meters, to enable the transmission of data or commands. Contactless cards generally have an onboard battery, and both reader and card have an internal antenna for secure communication.

## Smart Card Operating Systems

Because a smart card is a small computer, it has an onboard operating system designed to manage microprocessor tasks. These tasks include the following:

- Data transmission over the serial terminal interface
- Loading, operating, and managing applications
- Execution control and instruction processing
- Protected access to data
- Memory management
- File management
- Cryptographic algorithm execution

Three common and basic operating systems are found on smart cards:

- JavaCard operating system is developed by Sun Microsystems and promoted via the JavaCard forum. It is used for Java-based smart cards.
- MULTOS is a smart card operating system developed by a consortium led by MasterCard and Mondex. It is a multiapplication smart card operating system designed with high security for financial transactions.
- Windows for Smart Cards is a smart card operating system developed by Microsoft and designed for multiple applications.

### *Proximity Cards or RFID Cards*

Several companies are using proximity cards to control physical access. These proximity or RFID cards contain an internal antenna. When using this card, the employee holds his or her card within a few inches of the reader. The card reader receives a unique ID string from the card and transmits it to the central computer, which then tells the reader whether or not to open the door.

### *Combi Proximity Cards*

These cards integrate photo ID, proximity, magnetic stripe, and even smart card technology into a single card, so multiple cards for each function are not needed.

### *Hybrid Smart Cards*

A hybrid smart card has two chips embedded into the card's surface—one contact and one contactless—each with its own interface.

### *Combi Smart Cards*

Combi smart cards allow a single smart chip to securely interface with both contact and contactless readers.

# Applying Biometrics in Physical Security

In information technology, biometrics is the measurement and analysis of human fingerprints, irises, retinas, voices, faces, and hands. These measurements and their associated analyses are used in the process of authenticating individuals.

The implementation of biometrics can increase the overall security of an organization by removing reliance on passwords and the use of tokens that could be lost or shared. It also increases convenience, because users do not need to remember passwords or keep track of access cards.

## Biometric Process

There are two different parts of the biometric process, integrated into the same device and system. One of these parts is the biometric enrollment process, and the other is the biometric verification process. The following steps occur during the enrollment process:

1. The user provides the required nonbiometric data. This may include full name, address, account information, username, and password.
2. The user presents the raw biometric data. This may be through a scanning device, a camera, a microphone, or whatever acquisition device the biometric system is using.
3. The biometric device captures an image of the biometric data.
4. The biometric system processes the raw data and creates an enrollment template.
5. The enrollment template is stored with the required nonbiometric data for this user's account.

Once the user is registered in the system, the following steps can be taken to verify the identity of the user:

1. The user presents the raw biometric data.
2. The biometric device captures the biometric data.
3. The biometric system processes the raw data and creates a verification template.
4. The verification template is matched against the enrollment template.
5. The biometric system scores the degree of similarity between the enrollment and verification templates.
6. The biometric system checks to see if the score is above or below a defined threshold.
7. If the score is above the threshold, a match decision is made. If the score is below, a nonmatch decision is made.

## Accuracy of Biometrics

Accuracy of biometrics concerns the following three primary issues:

1. False match rate (FMR)

2. False nonmatch rate (FNMR)

3. Failure to enroll (FTE)

### False Match Rate (FMR)

This is the chance that the biometric scanner will falsely identify an unauthorized user as another, valid user.

### False Nonmatch Rate (FNMR)

This is the chance that the user's credentials provided at the time of authentication fail to match the data stored in the system. This is usually caused by the system having a greater detail of information than what is actually provided by the user.

### Failure to Enroll (FTE)

There is a chance that a user cannot enroll his or her biometric details into the system. There are several reasons for this, including an injured finger in fingerprint biometrics, a cataract in retinal scanning, and a sore throat in voice recognition.

## Biometrics Applications

The following are the some applications of biometrics:

- PC or network access
- Physical access
- Retail or ATM
- Criminal identification
- Citizen identification programs
- E-commerce

## Fingerprint Scanning

This is a popular technology related to biometrics. Many people associate the biometric technology of fingerprint scanning with that of the criminal fingerprint identification system, which can make them hesitant to enroll.

In the criminal fingerprint system, the entire fingerprint image is obtained and stored in a database and is printed when it is required. Biometric fingerprint scanning systems do not store a full image of a fingerprint in a database. Only a small template created from the fingerprint is stored. Fingerprint scanning devices can either be standalone devices or built into laptops, keyboards, or mice.

### Fingerprint Scanning Method

Fingerprint scanners are of two types: optical and capacitance. Optical scanners use a charged coupled device (CCD), which is the same as the light sensor used in some digital cameras and camcorders. CCD uses an array of specialized light-sensitive diodes called a *photosite*. When the scanner detects a finger, the CCD camera takes the picture.

A capacitance scanner is also used to capture an image of a fingerprint. But this scanner, instead of using light and a camera, uses electrical current to generate an image. This scanner contains tiny cells that house conductor plates. Each plate is smaller than the width of the single ridge of a fingerprint.

## Hand Geometry

Hand geometry is a biometric technique used to identify a user by the shape of his or her hand. It is a simple and accurate procedure. The use of this technique requires special hardware and can integrate into any system or device.

### Hand Geometric Process

The user places his or her hand on a metal surface. The device then verifies the user details in its database. This process takes less than 5 seconds.

## Voice Scanning

Scanning the human voice is one of the most common biometric technologies. This system uses voice recognition software to allow a user to interact with a computer by issuing commands verbally instead of using an input device such as a mouse.

### *Voice Scanning Process*

The voice scanning process is similar to other biometric technology. In this system, the raw biometric data is the sound waves produced by voice. This raw data is captured by different devices specifically made for voice scanning. The sound waves are converted from analog to digital early in the process. A microphone, landline telephone, cellular telephone, or any other device that can capture the human voice is suitable.

## Retinal Scanning

Even identical twins have different retinal patterns. The retina is a thin layer of nerves (about 0.5 mm thick) found on the back of the eye. The retina transmits impulses through the optic nerves to the brain.

Retinal scanning is difficult compared to other scanning in biometric technology. To present raw biometric data, users must move their head into position, with their eye very close (within an inch) to the scanner for it to read the retina through the pupil. During the scan process, the user focuses on a light in the scanner. After generating the template, this technique provides excellent matching.

## Iris Scanning

As with the retina, even twins also have different iris patterns. Some iris features include ligaments, furrows, striations, ridges, and zigzags. Iris scanning technology measures 247 independent variables in an iris. One of the most important applications of iris scanning is its use in bank ATMs for authentication.

Similar to fingerprint scanning, it also requires a device to capture the image and software to process the image. A camera uses infrared light to capture a high-resolution image. After capturing the image, the system locates the border between the pupil and the iris, which can be difficult for users with very dark irises. After noting the border, the system will convert the data to a grayscale image. The grayscale image is used to identify the unique features of the iris.

One example of an iris scanner is the Panasonic DT120, shown in Figure 1-1.

## Facial Scanning

Facial scanning or facial recognition is well known due to large-scale surveillance implementations. It works by picking out the unique characteristics of a human face and matching them against facial images in a database.

A facial scanning system looks at the following facial characteristics:

- Size of eyes
- Distance between the eyes

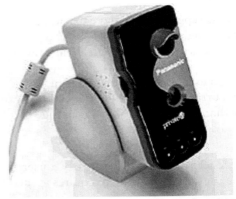

*Source:* http://www.eyenetwatch.com/iris/
panasonic-authenticam.htm. Accessed 2004.

**Figure 1-1**   The Panasonic DT120 is a small iris scanner for desktop computers.

- Depth of the eye sockets
- Location of the nose
- Size of the nose
- Location of the chin
- Size of the chin
- Jaw line
- Size, position, and shape of the cheekbones

### *Facial Scanning Process*

The facial scanning process starts with the acquisition of the raw biometric data: an image of a human face. This image can be acquired using any imaging source. The image should be of as high resolution as possible.

Once the system identifies the face, it will narrow in on the face and then record the image. After that, the image is scaled and rotated in order to align it with the processing software. The system will remove all extra data from the image such as hair, background images, and head so that the system can isolate only the face in the image.

After capturing the isolated facial image, the system will create a face print of that image. The face print is the template for the system.

# Implementing Workplace Security

It is common for both large and small companies to have areas where the majority of employees use computers at work. Sometimes, each of these employees has a cubicle for an office. Employees may like to personalize their workstations as well as their PCs, but they need to be educated on how to secure this personal space. People sometimes scribble their passwords, personal information, IP addresses, or telephone numbers on whiteboards, sticky notes, pads, or pieces of paper. This should be discouraged, since attackers can easily obtain this information, as well as critical information regarding the LAN and the company, by going through dumpsters or through other means. Address books, company policies, reminders, user IDs, etc., should be kept away from the reach of others.

The workstation can be physically secured in the following ways:

- CCTV cameras with monitored screens and video recorders can be used to monitor the movements of employees and visitors.
- Unmanned/unattended terminal screens should be locked to prevent unauthorized access.
- Workstation cubicles should be designed in such a way that employees cannot see each other's terminal screens.
- PCs should be locked down to prevent any physical movement.
- Removable media drives should be avoided as much as possible. Only one workstation per row should have such drives, and that particular workstation should not be used for any other purpose.

## Desktop Security

Managing desktop security includes people, processes, and technology factors.

### *People*

*Education and Awareness*   Users must be reminded of ways to avoid vulnerabilities. Threats faced by desktop users include:

- Programs that send clear (unencrypted) passwords
- Social-engineering attacks
- Virus attacks
- Unsolicited e-mail attachments
- Unattended desktops

- Packet sniffing
- Bad desktop management with no antivirus software, outdated virus signatures, and/or no backups

Some examples of education and awareness programs include:

- Regular seminars and road shows of security awareness
- Placing weekly posters on a bulletin board

*Enforcement* Security policies must be efficiently managed. Certain evidences must be present to properly claim a violation of policies, such as producing audit trails. If there is a serious security breach, efficient action must be taken with legal support.

## Processes

Strict adherence to the following processes set by the organization is essential to ensure desktop security:

- *IT security council*: The IT security council enables and designs the security policies and regularly checks the security process.
- *Policies*: Policies must be in place for things such as designing controls of application systems, developing user access controls, performing risk analysis, and conducting computer crime investigations.
- *Baselines*: These make sure systems are configured to security standards.
- *Procedures*: This is a detailed structure of the processes that go into completing a task.
- *User classification*: Dividing the users into different groups based on security needs allows administrators to have finer control and to manage user security in a more convenient and efficient way.
- *Reviews*: Security audits must be performed frequently by arranging seminars and reviews, so the user can correct errors before they are exploited.
- *Penetration testing*: Desktop security should be tested through penetration testing that involves various hacking techniques.

## Technology

The technologies involved in managing desktop security include:

- *Centralized management*: Client applications are not installed on the desktop. The user will be provided with only the data available on the desktop.
- *Password protection*: Passwords must be designed to be difficult to guess.
- *Single sign-on*: When an application contains multiple security features, there is a possibility that many passwords are available for a single user. This should be eliminated.
- *Desktop lock*: An attacker can view confidential files on an unlocked machine. A user should not leave the desktop unattended without locking it first.
- *Virus detection*: Antivirus software must be installed and regularly updated.
- *File encryption*: Encryption causes files to be inaccessible to unauthorized persons.
- *Personal firewall*: A firewall installed on a desktop PC increases security.

## Laptop Security

According to a survey conducted by the FBI in 2004, medium- and large-sized companies lose an average of 11.65 notebook computers a year by theft. If a laptop is lost, an organization should ask the following questions:

- What information of a strategic nature would be disclosed?
- What information of a tactical nature would be disclosed?
- What information about the company's network or computing infrastructure would be revealed that would facilitate an electronic attack?

## Laptop Security Measures

The following are some common laptop security measures:

- Encrypt sensitive data
- Back up everything on the laptop
- Trace the stolen laptop's location, if possible
- Set a BIOS password on the laptop
- Consider laptop PC insurance
- Add third-party privacy protection for highly sensitive data
- Use physical Kensington locks
- Use strong hardware-based security

## Laptop Lockers

Laptops can be secured with physical devices when they are stationary. This includes steel cable locks and tie-down bracelets.

## Portable Laptop Carts

Portable laptop carts provide mobility in school classrooms. It is easy to move the carts from classroom to classroom. Electrical units allow notebooks to be recharged while in the carts. The carts can be closed and locked to prevent unauthorized access to the laptops.

## Antitheft Tags

Antitheft tags affixed to laptops assist authorities in tracing stolen laptops found anywhere in the world.

## Tracking and Recovery Systems

Lost or stolen laptops can be recovered through a variety of tracking and recovery techniques.

*XTool Computer Tracker* XTool Computer Tracker offers portability and traceability. A software-based transmitter sends a signal to the Signal Control Center by means of a telephone or an Internet connection. This signal can track the location of the stolen piece of equipment. The signal enables the user to reboot the system when it starts and when the IP address changes. The user also has the ability to delete files remotely, even if the system is mobilized. Every signal holds the telephone number or the IP address that is used by the transmitted signal.

XTool Computer Tracker's features include the following:

- Supports Windows and Macintosh platforms
- Undetectable, even by some antivirus programs
- Can be upgraded or downgraded as needed without affecting the computer's security
- Adaptable to new environments or configurations
- Worldwide monitoring and recovery services

*zTrace Gold* zTrace Gold is an invisible software security application that traces the location of missing laptops. It is undetectable and cannot be erased. The computer completes a handshake with the zServer at every Internet connection. If the laptop is reported missing, the zTrace Recovery Team identifies the computer's exact physical location. The team then coordinates with local law enforcement for a completely outsourced recovery solution. For enterprises, zTrace Gold can be managed internally by an organization's own internal security department or outsourced to the zTrace Recovery Team.

*CyberAngel* Using its secure password entry system, the CyberAngel Windows software will alert registered users of any unauthorized access to that protected computer and lock the communication ports to prevent unauthorized users from accessing any outside networks. CyberAngel will also lock the sensitive data stored on that computer with some of the strongest encryption algorithms currently available. Protected files will be rendered invisible to the unauthorized user. When the client notifies the Security Monitoring Center that a registered computer has been stolen, the center can then locate the computer when it next reports an unauthorized access to the Security Monitoring Center.

*ComputracePlus*  ComputracePlus provides detailed tracking reports for any computer with an Internet connection.

# Securing Network Devices

## Server Security

The server is the most important component of any network, so it should be given a higher level of security. The server room should be well lit. A high-end configuration should be used for servers so that they can sustain the load caused by continuous uptime.

The server can be secured using the following means:

- Servers should not be used to perform day-to-day activities.
- Servers should be enclosed and locked to prevent any physical movement.
- Booting from floppy and CD-ROM drives on the server should be disabled and, if possible, these drives should not even be on the server.
- Some system administrators have a habit of labeling the server and other systems in the server room. These labels sometimes have the operating system's name and the server hardware specifications written on them. This is not advised, because anyone who passes through the server room can get details about the server and other devices. If an attacker sees this information, he or she does not have to go through the process of footprinting.
- Unnecessary services and subsystems should be removed.
- Server software should be updated regularly.

## Securing Backup Devices

When securing a network, data integrity is sometimes overlooked. It is important to maintain data integrity in systems and backups, which is the best defense against natural disasters, viruses, and hackers.

### Physical Access to the Boot CD-ROM and Floppy Drives

Physical access to a floppy drive or a CD-ROM on a domain controller or member server invites intrusion during the booting processes. Malicious users can use boot disks to completely delete data or even gain system access. The intruder can access the system and abort installation processes from the MS-DOS prompt.

### Removable Media

People use removable media in the workplace to store and move corporate information. Documents, databases, graphics, music, and video can be moved between computers using removable media, which are highly portable; thus, the security implications and risks of removable media need to be seriously assessed. Many high-security organizations like the military will prohibit the use or possession of removable media at their secure sites, often removing the availability of USB ports, floppy drives, and DVD/CD devices.

### Fax

It is important to apply great care when accepting a fax as genuine because its integrity is questionable; there is no data validation or authentication between sender and receiver. Every fax machine can use the Calling Station Identifier (CSID) if required, while some software can check the names of CSID during the transmission. Faxes should not be used for secret information.

## Personnel Security Practices and Procedures

The following procedures are involved in personnel security:

- A screening process is established to determine an employee's background. The background check includes criminal and financial screening. Education, past experience, and other qualifications are verified during screening.

- An employee access card is used to allow authorized persons into the office.
- An employee should complete access agreements before accessing any system. They may include confidentiality/nondisclosure agreements, acceptable-use agreements, user rules of behavior, and conflict-of-interest agreements.
- A formal sanction process has to be planned for personnel failing to act in accordance with established information security policies and procedures. The process should be in agreement with related federal laws, directives, policies, regulations, standards, and guidance.
- IT personnel security requirements for third-party providers should be established. Third-party providers include the following:
  - Service bureaus
  - Contractors
  - Information technology services
  - Outsourced applications
  - Network and security management

## Position Sensitivity

Before a person is given a sensitive position, a security investigation is performed and then the person is granted the applicable clearance level. The following are the appropriate codes for position sensitivity names:

- Nonsensitive
- Noncritical sensitive
- Critical sensitive
- Special sensitive
- Moderate risk
- High risk

## Employee Clearance

The following are the steps to relieve an employee of his or her responsibilities:

- An employee has to submit a resignation or retirement letter to the department head with a copy to the HR (Human Resources) Department. The department head will forward that resignation letter to the central leave coordinator.
- After receiving the resignation letter from an employee, the department head will set the last working date of that employee.
- The employee should fill out the clearance form and also have a meeting with the central leave coordinator from the HR Department to provide a plan for the last working days.
- After having a chat with that employee, the HR department will send a notice to obtain clearance from all the departments specified in the clearance form.
- After receiving the notice from the HR Department, all departments will send the due certificates to the central leave coordinator.
- The employee should contact the central leave coordinator during the last day in order to complete the clearance process.
- After verifying all the clearance certificates from all the departments, the central leave coordinator will clear the employee through a clearance form.
- After getting all the clearance certificates, the central leave coordinator will provide the employee with the following forms:
  - W-2 change of address form
  - Insurance form
  - Exit interview form (optional)
- The central leave coordinator will sign the clearance form, which depends on the clearance certificates from all the departments.

## Access Authorization

Access authorization allows an employee to enter the office only with the appropriate access card. This is meant to protect important data and the entire building from unauthorized physical access. It also protects the equipment from unauthorized physical access, tampering, and theft. The employee must give his or her access card back to the head of the department or to HR when leaving.

The following are the advantages of access authorization:

- Does not allow access to unauthorized persons
- Provides details about employees who have entered the office
- Prevents data loss from physical access

## Systems Maintenance Personnel

System maintenance requires both physical and logical access to the system. There are too many systems that have maintenance accounts. Companies preconfigure these accounts with specific and widely known passwords. The most common method hackers use to break into systems is through maintenance accounts that contain guessable passwords. IT personnel should change the password frequently and deactivate unused accounts. The developed procedure should allow only authorized maintenance personnel to access those accounts.

A maintenance manual assists in defining the characteristics and responsibilities of system maintenance personnel. It also provides maintenance personnel with the information required to do their job. The administrator should monitor the maintenance personnel.

Support and operations include the following:

- User support
- Software support
- Configuration management
- Backups
- Media controls
- Documentation
- Maintenance

Maintenance includes the following:

- Managing time settings with automatic update, time zone, and daylight saving time
- Managing backup frequency, personal computer settings, and office safe settings
- Managing feature keys to provide other capabilities
- Providing tools to exhibit network diagnostic and advanced troubleshooting tools
- Giving directions to update systems
- Restarting with the following options:
  - Normal restart
  - Restart with factory defaults restored
  - Restart in safe mode

## Contractors

Contractors should have an office identity card with photo and personal details, perhaps with a defined period of validity. All contractors should carry their ID cards at all times. Contractors must exhibit their ID cards clearly to the security officer. Contractors should return their ID cards when they are terminated or when they resign.

# CCTV (Closed-Circuit Televisions)

CCTV cameras help analyze the events of the day, in case something suspicious happens. They provide real-time monitoring of the premises. Simply having them present and displayed can act as a deterrent. The only drawback of these cameras is that their usefulness depends on the personnel monitoring them.

## Parking Area

The parking should be safe and secure. It should be surrounded by a boundary of some sort and should be guarded.

## EPS (Electronic Physical Security)

EPS (electronic physical security) is the integrated application of a number of electronic security systems. This includes the following:

- Addressable fire detection systems
- Automatic gas suppression systems
- CCTV systems
- RFID, biometric, and smart card access control systems
- Intrusion detection systems
- Law enforcement systems and products
- Guarding equipment and a guarding plan

# Understanding the Challenges in Ensuring Physical Security

### Enforcing Physical Security Policy

Practical problems, such as inconveniences caused by the implementation of physical security policies, may raise security threats.

### Social-Engineering Attempts

Social-engineering tricks may be attempted to trick personnel into divulging sensitive information. Such knowledge may prompt attackers to find ways to compromise security systems. Management should provide enough training to employees to make them aware of social-engineering attempts.

### Restrictions for Sharing Experience and Knowledge

Access control policies may restrict personnel in one department from sharing their experiences and knowledge with other departments. Physical security ensures data security but may also restrict knowledge and experience sharing.

### Cost and Time

Installing a physical security department in a company takes both time and money. Costs are incurred in the form of salaries, system installations, training, and more. Management can also outsource security functions to a firm that specializes in this area.

### Sophisticated Technologies

Physical security personnel often counter problems with sophisticated technologies. Visitors may carry a spy camera with them to take pictures of the target company, voice recorders for eavesdropping, etc. Security personnel should be trained regularly on these technologies.

# Physical Security Measures

### Fences

Fences can be used as a deterrent. A high-security installation must contain two fences—an outer and inner fence, each between 15 and 30 feet high.

### Guards

Guards can determine what action to take in each circumstance as it comes along and to make logical responses. Most guards have definite standard operating procedures (SOPs) that assist them in unknown situations.

## Dogs

Dogs can be an important part of physical security if they are included in the plan appropriately and administered properly. Their keen senses of smell and hearing can identify breaches that human guards cannot.

## Locks and Keys

In addition to standard mechanical locks, electromechanical locks can accept a range of inputs such as magnetic strips or ID cards, radio signals from name badges, PINs typed into a keypad, or a combination of these.

Manual locks are installed in doors and cannot be altered except by an expert locksmith. They are meant for restricting access to a single door. Programmable locks, on the other hand, can be changed after they have been used, without a locksmith.

## Locking Down USB Ports

Sometimes, it may be necessary to lock or disable the USB ports on a system to prevent unauthorized use. If a USB storage device is not already installed on the computer, the administrator can assign the user or group "deny permission" via the following files:

- %SystemRoot%\Inf\Usbstor.pnf
- %SystemRoot%\Inf\Usbstor.inf

In order to do this, follow these steps:

1. Locate the **%SystemRoot%\Inf** folder.
2. Right-click the **Usbstor.pnf** file, and then click **Properties**.
3. Click the **Security** tab.
4. In the **Group** or **User names** list, click the user or group that you want to set "deny permission" for.
5. In the **Permissions for UserName or GroupName** list, check the **Deny** check box, and then click the **OK** button.

In addition, add the System account to the **Deny** list. Repeat the above steps for the **Usbstor.inf** file as well.

## DeviceLock

DeviceLock is a device control solution designed to safeguard network computers against internal and external attacks. It is shown in Figure 1-2, and its features include the following:

- Network administrators can lock out unauthorized users from USB.
- Administrators can control access to any device such as floppies, serial and parallel ports, optical disc drives, and USB devices.
- Users can generate a report concerning the permissions that have been set.
- Provides a level of precision control over available device resources.
- Grants users temporary access to USB devices when there is no network connection.
- Allows the system to be controlled remotely using the centralized management console.
- Generates a report displaying the USB, FireWire, and PCMCIA devices.
- Sets devices in read-only mode.
- Gives a complete log of port and device activity, such as uploading and downloading, made by users and filenames in the standard Windows Event Log.

## Trackstick GPS Tracking Device

The Trackstick GPS Tracking Device is a 1 MB memory stick that can store months of travel information. It has the capability to record the following:

- Time
- Date

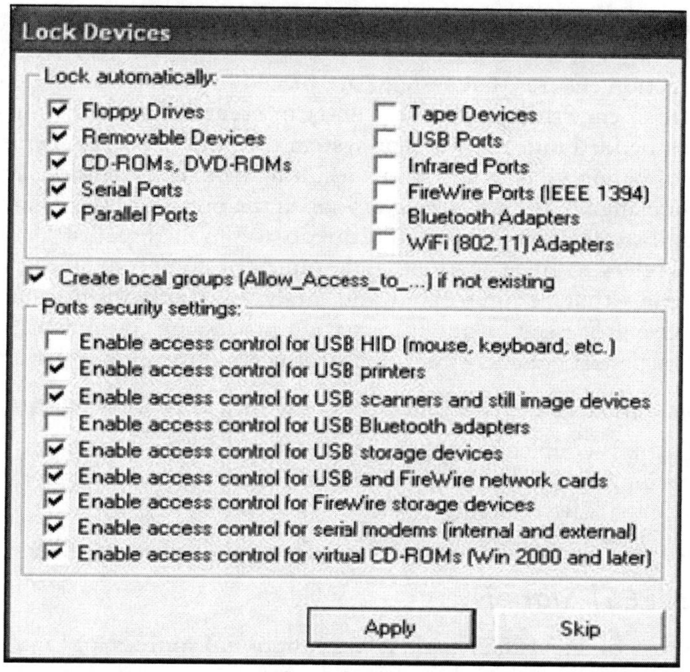

*Source:* http://www.devicelock.com/. Accessed 2004.

**Figure 1-2** DeviceLock can automatically lock devices.

- Speed
- Direction
- Altitude

The output comes in the following formats:

- RTF
- XLS
- HTML
- Google Earth KML

The Trackstick receives signals from 24 satellites orbiting Earth and works from anywhere on the planet. A specially designed algorithm can measure the time, even indoors. The Trackstick has the ability to map the time and location accurately. Each location can be pinpointed within 15 meters.

## USB Tokens

In large organizations that have shared computers, USB tokens can be used to establish a VPN tunnel. There is no need to reconfigure the computers to set up a VPN tunnel if a USB token is used. A PIN has to be entered each time the device is plugged in.

## TEMPEST

All electronic devices, including computers, have emanations that can be captured and monitored from a distance. In the case of computers, data flow could be compromised by simply intercepting these electromagnetic radiation (EMR) emanations. Thus, TEMPEST was born. At first it was a secret military project, and it is still illegal to possess TEMPEST-type monitoring devices. TEMPEST can be short for either Transient Electromagnetic Pulse Emanation Surveillance Technology or Telecommunication Electronics Protected from Emanating Spurious Transmissions, though there is no official definition or meaning. These emanations can be of electrical, mechanical, or acoustical energy, all of which can now, with modern technology, be captured. TEMPEST monitoring can involve protecting against unauthorized eavesdropping or the capturing and interpretation of such information.

TEMPEST protection ensures that systems are placed in protected and secure areas, such as a *Faraday cage* (a metallic enclosure or cage that prevents the entry or escape of an electromagnetic field by having a fine-mesh copper screening embedded into the walls or system container), and implements other security measures, such as the elimination of windows. The vibrations resulting from conversations taking place inside a room can now be monitored by focusing a laser measuring device on the outside glass. There are a number of methods used to protect systems against these emanations and threats to physical security.

TEMPEST also refers to investigations and studies of compromising emanations (CE) that include unintentionally sent signals that, if intercepted and analyzed, disclose information that is transmitted, received, handled, or otherwise processed by any information processing equipment.

CE is electrical or acoustical energy emitted by any equipment or system. CE can also occur as:

- Electromagnetic fields emitted by elements of plaintext processing equipment
- Text-related signals coupled to cipher, power, signal, control, or other BLACK (normal unsecured circuits and equipment) lines through common circuit elements such as grounds and power supplies or inductive and capacitive coupling
- Sound waves from mechanical or electromechanical devices, or the human voice

### Sources of TEMPEST Signals

The two basic sources of TEMPEST signals are functional sources and incidental sources. Functional sources generate electromagnetic energy, while incidental sources are not designed to generate electromagnetic energy.

The CE sources include all electromechanical and electronic equipment and systems. The extent of CE must be determined, and necessary countermeasures must be applied to the equipment.

### Types of TEMPEST Signals

Electrical conductors connected to circuits having the same impedance and power source as equipment processing RED baseband signals can introduce RED baseband emanations. It can be introduced into escape media by capacitive or inductive coupling and by radiation with RED baseband signals of higher frequencies or data rates.

Modulated spurious carriers are the results of modulation arising in a carrier because of RED data. Impulsive emanations are caused by very fast digital signal transitions. Impulsive emanations can be radiated into space or coupled with the external conductors of the equipment under test.

### Shielding

TEMPEST shielding helps protect devices from electromagnetic radiation. Corporations also use it to prevent information loss. To reduce TEMPEST emanations, most devices use newly designed microcomponents. Communication security provides low-cost service by reducing the shielded volume to the required size for the protection of RED equipment. The cost of the shielding solution is based on the type of system to be protected. Shielding volumes are classified into two types:

- Small volumes are known as shielded enclosures and do not require protection from the overall facility structure.
- Large volumes are known as shielded areas and are concentrated on the main part of the facility and mostly require integration into the structural design.

### Grounding

Grounding supplies a low-resistance path that moves lightning, power transients, and emanations to the reference point. The system is made up of an earth electrode subsystem (EESS), a fault protection subsystem (FPSS), a signal reference subsystem, and a lightning protection subsystem:

- The earth electrode subsystem has a maximum resistance of 10 ohms.
- The fault protection subsystem (FPSS) is intended to shield personnel and equipment from electrical circuit faults.
- The lightning protection subsystem provides protection against lightning and other temporary voltages that may enter the building.
- The signal reference subsystem provides a common signal ground reference for the entire building.

By grounding RED/BLACK signals, signal grounds, EESS grounds, cable ladders, conduits, and ducts can be connected. An equipotential ground plane is frequently installed in secure facilities to minimize the results of compromising emanations. This consists of the following equipment:

- Distribution frames
- Patch panels
- RED/BLACK processing

### Attenuation

EMI shielding is calculated in decibels of attenuation. Shielding is more effective as the dB of the attenuation increases. The signal strength is calculated as the ratio of the signal strength in the clear to the signal strength through the shield.

### Banding

Banding refers to restricting information to a specific set of frequencies, thus protecting information from being hacked. If banding is not properly done, then there is a chance of impartial data loss.

### Filtered Power

Filtered power filters out the redundant electromagnetic radiations from equipment. Generally, low-pass filters can prevent everything, excluding high-frequency signals. Low-pass filters are restricted under high-frequency signals. The core function of the TEMPEST filter is to prevent the radiation of RED signals. However, filters are not able to reduce unintended emissions to zero.

### Cabling

The TEMPEST emission control standard for network cabling systems combined with data encryption and other security systems enable information security. Fiber optic cable radiates only heat emissions, but it is costlier than copper cable. According to TEMPEST standards, potential emanations are generally addressed by placing all cables inside a ferrous channel or tubing to block any electromagnetic radiation.

The shielded copper cable will provide an additional layer of security that reduces some emissions. Single overall shielded (FTP) cables, like the one pictured in Figure 1-3, do not eliminate the need for conduit and RED/BLACK separation in high-security environments. The separation distance is lower with shielded cables, decreasing the cost for pathways and spaces.

The Siemon's TERA end-to-end network cabling system uses S/FTP cable and fully shielded connectivity, and was the first copper network cabling system to pass NSA-certified TEMPEST security testing. In S/FTP cable, each pair is shielded separately and an overall braid shield surrounds all connectors. This shielding removes the potential security gap caused by single radiation or emission. The additional shielding that is combined into the outlets and plugs eliminates all potential emissions from the overall cabling system.

S/FTP shielded twisted-pair cabling consists of the following:

- Conductor
- Insulation

*Source:* www.siemon.com/shielded-twistedpair.asp. Accessed 2004.

**Figure 1-3**   This is a cross section of an S/FTP cabling system.

- Tinned copper braid
- Aluminum/polyester foil tape
- Outer jacket

### Zoning

Zoning is a control method used when different protection levels are required. A damaged UPS and communication room should have a medium protection level area, such as 60 decibels, while a damaged control and computer room should have a high protection level area, perhaps 100 decibels. The zones can be used to show the main form and features of different areas. Generally, the weakest areas are located at the center, inside other areas.

Zones are categorized into the following areas:

- Zone 0 is for protected areas.
- Zone 1 is for the generator area.
- Zone 2 is for the UPS and communication area.
- Zone 3 is for complicated control rooms.

### TEMPEST Separation

Isolators are used to isolate, through attenuation or insertion, loss between a source and a load. It works like a filter but its isolator characteristics are very high. Circuit isolation reaches its destination by using transformers, feedback amplifiers, or optical couplers. Isolators provide an open circuit to unwanted signals. An isolator should have a minimum of a 4-inch optically coupled path to meet TEMPEST requirements, subject to the stress isolators that are connected to the lines carrying lightning or EMP transients.

Encryption safeguards confidential information from being exposed. Unwanted emanations from RED equipment that occur due to interceptions cannot be prevented via encryption. There are several steps that equipment and facility designers can take to prevent information exposure through compromised emanations. All these techniques minimize the potential of a stray signal and involve hiding the sensitive content in the background electrical noise.

## Fire Safety: Fire Suppression, Gaseous Emission Systems

### Portable System

These are used when direct implementation of fire suppression is required. They are effective for smaller fires, and they prevent the activation of a building's sprinkler systems, which would likely cause water damage. Portable systems are rated by the type of fire they are designed to suppress:

- Class A interrupts the ability of the fuel to be ignited. This is best for fire caused by normal combustible fuels such as wood, paper, and textiles.
- Class B removes oxygen from the fire. This is best for fire caused by combustible liquids or gases. Carbon dioxide, multipurpose dry chemicals, and halon fire extinguishers are best suited for these types.
- Class C uses nonconducting agents. This is best for fire caused by powerful electrical equipment. They use nonconducting agents, such as carbon dioxide, multipurpose dry chemicals, and halon.
- Class D uses special agents for combustible metal fires, such as those involving magnesium, lithium, and sodium.

### Gaseous System

*Dry-Pipe System*   The dry-pipe system is intended to work in areas hosting electrical machinery. It contains pressurized air. This air keeps the valves closed and escapes through the sprinkler heads. This decreases the threat of accidental initiation of the system. It is the best solution for advanced computer environments.

*Preaction System*   This system has a two-phase reaction to fire. When fire is detected, the first phase is triggered and valves allow water to enter the system. A difference between the preaction system and the deluge system is that, in the deluge system, valves are left open as soon as the first phase is triggered, without waiting for the second phase to begin.

## Gaseous Emission Systems

Chemical gas systems that suppress fires have a supplementary agent. There are two major types of gaseous systems: carbon dioxide and halon. Carbon dioxide absorbs the oxygen supply to the fire. Halon is a cleaning agent that does not leave any filtrate when dry and also does not interfere with electronic equipment. Carbon dioxide has the dangerous side effect of possible suffocation, and halon can deplete the ozone layer.

The following are some alternative agents:

- *FM-200*: Identical to halon 1301 and safe in residential areas
- *Inergen*: Combination of nitrogen, argon, and carbon dioxide
- *FE-13*: A more recent and safer cleaning agent

## Fire Detection

Fire detection systems are either manual or automatic. Manual systems consist of human reactions, such as calling the fire department, while automatic systems have physically activated alarms, such as sprinklers and gaseous systems.

## Thermal Detection

Thermal detection systems contain an advanced heat detector that functions in either of two ways. The first is called fixed temperature. Here, the sensor recognizes when the environmental temperature reaches a preset level, perhaps around 135° Fahrenheit or 57° Celsius. The second is called rate of rise. Here, the sensor detects an abnormal increase in the environmental temperature within a short period of time.

## Smoke Detection

This is a common way of detecting fire in residential as well as commercial buildings. Smoke detectors function in three ways. In the first, photoelectric sensors detect an infrared beam in an area. In the second, an ionization sensor contains a small quantity of injurious radioactive material inside a detection chamber. Air-aspirating detectors are very advanced and are used in high-sensitivity areas. They function by taking in air and passing it through a compartment containing a laser beam. If the laser beam is diverted by smoke, the system is initiated.

## Flame Detector

This detects the infrared or UV light created by an open flame. Flame detectors need a direct line of sight with the flame. They match the flame signature against a database to determine whether to trigger the alarm and suppression systems.

# Heating, Ventilation, and Air Conditioning

## Temperature

Computer systems are liable to get damaged from abnormally high temperatures. At 175°F, hardware can be damaged or destroyed. At 32°F, media are vulnerable to cracking and the components can freeze.

Rapid fluctuations in temperature can generate short circuits or otherwise harm a system and its components. The optimal temperature for a computer is between 70°F and 74°F.

## Humidity

High humidity levels lead to condensation problems, and low levels can increase the quantity of static electricity. This can short-circuit electrical equipment, and fungus can grow and rot paper.

## Ventilation Shafts

In residences, the ductwork can be big enough for intruders to climb through. In many buildings, the shafts can be entirely outside the view of security personnel. In most buildings, the vents lead to separate rooms and are no larger than 12–24 inches. If the vents are much bigger, security can use wire mesh grids at different places.

## Power Management and Conditioning

### Grounding

Grounding guarantees that electric current is appropriately discharged to the ground. If a piece of electrical equipment is not properly grounded, any user touching that equipment might get an electric shock, and the equipment can be damaged. In rare cases, this can even lead to death. Electrical equipment installed in regions that have contact with water must be carefully grounded with GFCI equipment (ground fault circuit interruption). GFCI has the ability to rapidly identify and obstruct a ground defect. Power must also be provided in adequate amperage to sustain the required operations. Overburdening a circuit can overburden the power load on an electrical cable, possibly causing a fire.

### Emergency Shutoff

Most computer rooms and wiring closets are built with an emergency power shutoff in the form of a large, obvious red button. Such devices are a last resort to prevent personal damage and machine damage during flooding or sprinkler activation.

### Water Problems

Absence of water causes problems for fire suppression systems and cooling systems. On the other hand, too much water can be a major threat. Damage due to water can cause computers and other electrical equipment to fail. Therefore, flooding and leaks must be prevented, as they may cause damage to paper and electronic information storage.

### Structural Collapse

Inescapable environmental factors cause buildings to collapse. Buildings are designed and built with definite load restrictions, and overloading the capacity can lead to structural failure. Regular inspections by expert civil engineers are necessary.

### Uninterruptible Power Supplies

In incidents of power failure, a UPS acts as a backup for important computer systems.

### Standby or Offline UPS

A standby or offline UPS is an offline battery backup that recognizes when power is no longer supplied from the electrical service. When this happens, the UPS transfers power from its batteries through a DC-to-AC converter until the power is recovered or the computer shuts down.

### Ferroresonant Standby UPS

A ferroresonant standby UPS enhances the standard UPS design. The major difference is that it substitutes the UPS transfer switch. The transformer performs power conditioning and line filtering on the major power source, decreasing the effect of power problems. The transformer also stores energy in its coils, offering a buffer to fill the deficit between the break in the power supply and activation of the battery backup. This reduces the chances of system reset and data loss. These are best suited to a setting that demands a huge capacity of conditioned and genuine power, as they can go up to 14,000 VA.

### Line-Interactive UPS

A line-interactive UPS has a considerably different design than the others. The inner components of the standby models are substituted with a pair of inverters and converters. Its major power source is from the main line, with the battery as the support. As soon as the power supply is stopped, the inverters and converters begin providing the power. Since the device is connected to the output, this model has a quicker response time and has built-in power conditioning and line filtering.

### True-Online UPS

True-online UPS is the most expensive type. The process frequently changes from an AC to DC battery storage and continues to be AC fed, generating high quantities of heat. An advanced model resolves this problem by hosting a delta-conversion unit that permits some of the inward power to be fed directly to target computers,

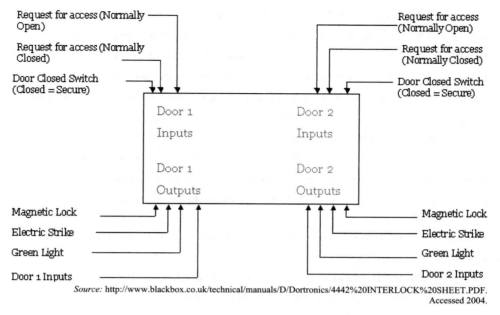

*Source:* http://www.blackbox.co.uk/technical/manuals/D/Dortronics/4442%20INTERLOCK%20SHEET.PDF.
Accessed 2004.

**Figure 1-4**   This is the programming logic for a mantrap system.

decreasing the quantity of energy wasted and heat produced. If the power supply ceases, the delta unit shuts off and batteries mechanically balance the high power needed, but the systems continue and do not recognize a fluctuation in voltage levels.

## Mantrap

A mantrap offers alternate access to resources. It has two different doors with an airlock between them. A single door can be opened at a time, and authentication is required for both doors.

Mantraps restrict access to secure areas within a facility while providing an effective means to physically detain unauthorized persons until security provides clearance. Mantraps are typically manual swing doors forming a vestibule, but they can also use sliding doors or gates. Some mantraps make use of turnstiles or revolving doors.

Once a person gets into the first door, he or she is not allowed to enter the second door until the first one is closed.

This system offers protection in three ways:

- It is difficult to forcibly enter through a single door.
- It permits time to evaluate the person inside the mantrap prior to letting him or her enter the second door.
- It permits only one person to enter at a time.

In huge systems like those available in government installations and large financial institutions, many doors can be installed to create a massive mantrap system. Figure 1-4 shows the programming logic for a mantrap.

# Developing a Physical Security Checklist

A physical security checklist defines the areas that need to be secured. It also describes the methods, technologies, and applications used to ensure that security.

Physical security protects:

- Stored information resources of the company
- Functions of the information systems

A security checklist should include the following steps:

1. Examine and analyze the buildings and boundaries that are problematic.
2. Install strong windows and locks on the doors, and ensure that the doors remain locked.
3. Place servers and other important assets in secured rooms without windows.
4. Set up proper air conditioners and fire detecting systems in the rooms where servers are located.
5. Keep important resources away from vents, pipes, toilets, radiators, and insecure zones.
6. Turn off monitor screens at night.
7. Maintain an inventory list, including memory, processors, serial numbers, locations, and purchase dates.
8. Label critical resources by using ultraviolet marking, which aids in the recovery of lost and stolen materials.
9. Maintain a backup of data and store it far from the source machines. Storing the backups off site is the best solution.
10. Distributing computers across multiple sites secures data from theft.
11. Physically lock equipment in open areas.
12. Carrying identification cards ensures that no outsider enters the organization without being noticed.
13. Ensure that visitors are genuine at the reception area.

## Chapter Summary

- In addition to securing the network from external software attacks, the physical security of assets must be ensured.
- Both human (e.g., vandals, disgruntled employees, and attackers) and natural factors (e.g., earthquakes, floods, and electrical storms) affect the physical security of an organization.
- Some unsecured places where office information can be found are workstations, work areas, dustbins, and monitors.
- A smart card is a credit card–sized plastic device that contains a computer chip and memory. It can store, process, and output data securely.
- In information technology, biometrics is the measurement and analysis of human fingerprints, irises, retinas, voices, faces, and hands.
- Managing desktop security includes people, processes, and technology factors.
- Improving physical security involves both physical and technological solutions.

## Review Questions

1. What is physical security?

2. Who is responsible for physical security?

3.  What factors affect physical security?

_____

_____

_____

_____

4.  What are the different types of attackers?

_____

_____

_____

_____

5.  How do you implement premises security?

_____

_____

_____

_____

6.  What are smart cards?

_____

_____

_____

_____

7.  Explain the process of fingerprint scanning.

_____

_____

_____

_____

8.  What are some laptop security procedures?

_____

_____

_____

_____

9.  Explain the process of securing backups.

_____

_____

_____

_____

10. How does a mantrap work?

_____

_____

_____

_____

# Hands-On Projects

1. Use 1st Security Agent to password-protect and secure Windows-based computers.

   ▪ Navigate to Chapter 1 of the Student Resource Center.

   ▪ Install and launch the 1st Security Agent program.

   ▪ Click **Screen Lock** under User Restrictions, check the **Screen-lock Password** check box, and then click **Change**.

   ▪ Change the password and click the **OK** button.

   ▪ Go to the Control Panel option in User Restrictions, click **Add or Remove**, and check the **Disable Add/Remove Programs** check box.

   ▪ Go to the Explorer option in User Restrictions, check the **Hide Drives in My Computer** check box, and select the drives to be hidden.

   ▪ Go to the Start Menu option in User Restrictions and check the **Remove My Network Places from the Start Menu** check box.

   ▪ Go to the Taskbar option in User Restrictions and check the **Hide the Taskbar Clock** check box.

   ▪ Go to the Special Icons option in User Restrictions and check the **Hide My Computer Icon** check box.

   ▪ Go to the menu bar, click **Apply Tree**, and click the **OK** button in the **Confirm** window to apply the settings.

   ▪ To remove all restrictions, click **Clear Tree** in the menu bar and click the **OK** button in the **Confirm** window.

2. Use Access Lock to secure your desktop when you are away from your computer.

   ▪ Navigate to Chapter 1 of the Student Resource Center.

   ▪ Install and launch the Access Lock program.

   ▪ Click the **Options** icon in the menu bar. A new window will be opened. Click the **Screen Saver** tab and check the **Lock screen** option.

   ▪ Go to the **Security** tab in the Options window and check the check boxes as desired.

   ▪ Click **Password** on the menu bar, type the desired password, and click the **OK** button to change the password.

   ▪ Click **Activate** in the menu bar to make these settings active.

   ▪ Click **Deactivate** in the menu bar to deactivate the settings.

3. Use Access Denied XP to safeguard your computer from unwanted access and protect the desktop and boot process.

   ▪ Navigate to Chapter 1 of the Student Resource Center.

   ▪ Install and launch the Access Denied XP program.

   ▪ Click the plus icon in the menu bar to add a new user account.

   ▪ Enter the user information in the Add User account window and click the **OK** button.

■ Click the users icon in the menu bar, as shown in Figure 1-5, to manage user accounts.

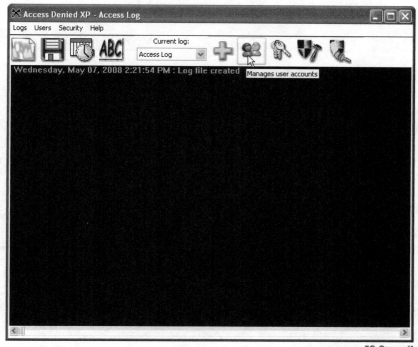

**Figure 1-5**   This is the users icon.

■ Select the user account you wish to modify, type the user information, and click the **OK** button.

■ Click the security icon, as shown in Figure 1-6, in the menu bar to set the security options.

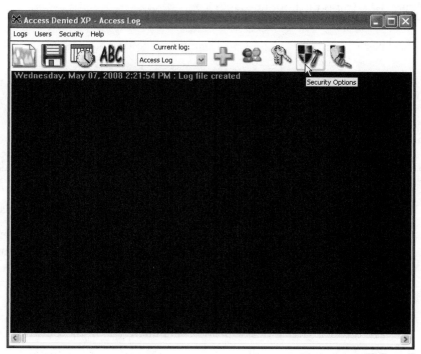

**Figure 1-6**   This is the security icon.

- Set the security settings as desired and click the **OK** button to activate.
- Click the boot messages icon, shown in Figure 1-7, in the menu bar to edit boot messages.

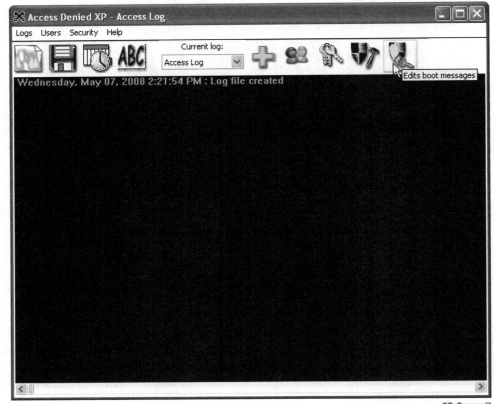

**Figure 1-7**   This is the boot messages icon.

- Set the settings in the **Edit Logon Access Messages** window and click **Test** to check the view of the login screen.

4. Use Desktop Lock to lock the PC and protect it from unauthorized access.

- Navigate to Chapter 1 of the Student Resource Center.
- Install and launch the Desktop Lock program.
- To set the desktop lock settings, click **Configure**.
- To set the Lock Mode settings, click the **Lock** tab and select the desired options.
- To set the Unlock Mode settings, click the **Unlock** tab and select the desired options.
- To set the display options while the system is locked, click the **Display** tab.
- To set the advanced options, click the **Advanced** tab and select the desired options.
- To set up the schedule items, click the **Schedule** tab and click **Setup**.
- To set up the user mode settings, click the **Users** tab.
- Click the **OK** button to apply the settings.
- Click the **Lock Now** button to lock the desktop.
- To create a virtual desktop, click **Virtual Screen** in the **Desktop Lock** window.
- Click **Options** to set the virtual screen options in the **Virtual Screen** window.

- Click **Profiles Manager** to manage profiles.
- To add a profile name, click **Add** in the profiles manager of the **Virtual Screen** window.
- Enter the profile name in the **Input profile name** window and click the **OK** button.
- To change or set the password for the profile, click **Change** in the **Profile Settings** window.
- Enter the password and click the **OK** button in the **Set Password** window.
- Click **OK** in the **Profile Settings** window to apply the profile settings.
- To quit the application, click **Exit**.

5. Use Lockdown Plus PC to prevent users from deleting critical files and applications, making unauthorized changes to the desktop, saving unwanted programs, running disallowed programs, and downloading using Internet Explorer.

- Navigate to Chapter 1 of the Student Resource Center.
- Install and launch the Lockdown Plus PC program.
- To protect files and folders, click the **Protect Files and Folders** option, and then start the wizard by clicking the **Wizard** button.
- Select a desired option for securing the objects and click **Next**.
- Click **Add Files** to add the files to be protected.
- Browse the files in the location that you want to protect and click **Open**.
- Click **Lock** to apply the protection.
- Click **Unlock** to remove the file restrictions.
- To protect the local hard disks, click **Protect Local Hard Disks**.
- Select the drive you wish to lock, set the desired options, and click **Lock** to lock the hard drive.
- Click **Unlock** to unlock the disk protection.
- To restrict external drives, click **Restrict External Drives**.
- Select the device name and click **Lock** to restrict access.
- Click **Protect Window System** to select the settings for restricting access to the Windows system.
- Click **Manage Accounts** to manage user accounts.
- To change the password, click **Password**, enter the desired password, and click the **OK** button.

Chapter **2**

# Firewalls

## Objectives

**After completing this chapter, you should be able to:**

- Understand the basic components of a firewall
- Differentiate between firewall types
- Understand firewall configuration strategies
- Secure against hacking by using a firewall
- Understand the concept of a DMZ
- Understand firewall limitations
- Conduct firewall log analysis
- Select appropriate firewall tools

## Key Terms

**DMZ (demilitarized zone)**   a zone that resides outside an internal network and offers open access to servers such as Web servers and host-and-router setups

**Firewall**   a program or machine placed at a network gateway server that helps protect a private network from users of a different network

**Hardware firewall**   a dedicated device that is meant only for firewalling

**Network address translation (NAT)**   a process used to change the IP address on a packet to a different IP address relevant to another network

**Network address translation (NAT) software**   software that separates IP addresses into two sets, enabling LANs to use the addresses for internal and external traffic

**Screening routers**   routers that perform packet filtering between the client systems and the Internet

**Software firewalls**   pieces of software that sit between the user applications and the networking components of the operating system

**Specialty firewalls**   firewalls built to secure specific network communications

# Introduction to Firewalls

A *firewall* is a program placed at a network gateway server that helps protect a private network from the users of a different network. A firewall can also be a secure, reliable, and trusted machine placed between private and public networks. Firewalls are configured with a set of rules to trace network traffic and are responsible for allowing the traffic to be passed or refused. They are also placed inside an organization to protect different departments within the organization. This chapter covers the following aspects of firewalls:

- Security features, components, and operations
- Types and functionality, including PIX firewalls
- Configuration strategies
- Scalability and architecture of firewalls based on dual-homed, screened-host, and screened-subnet configurations
- Threats and security risks
- Network protection from hacking
- Deployment strategies of firewalls and firewalls within routers
- DMZs
- Limitations of firewalls
- Firewall logs
- Firewall tools

# Firewall Features

## Security Features

Most firewalls can perform the following security functions:

- Logging unauthorized and authorized access both in and out of a network
- Providing a virtual private network (VPN) link to another network
- Authenticating users who provide usernames and passwords for identification, and enabling access to the services they need
- Protecting hosts within the network so that hackers cannot identify them and use them as staging areas for attacks
- Caching data for files that are repeatedly requested; data can be called from the cache to reduce the server load and improve Web site performance
- Filtering content considered inappropriate, such as video streams or executable e-mail attachments

### *Perimeter Security for Networks*

A firewall provides perimeter security, because it functions on the outer boundary, or perimeter, of a network. The network boundaries are where the network connection is able to reach another network. Firewalls act as checkpoints on the perimeter of the network to provide protection. A firewall located at the perimeter of a network provides the following advantages:

- Enables checkpoints that block viruses and infected e-mail messages from entering
- Logs traffic and protects the network from traffic entering all at once
- Reduces the damage to the network when an attack occurs
- Enables security for all the computers on a network so that an individual workstation does not require its own security

## Components of a Firewall

A firewall consists of many different components. The following components can make up a firewall:

- *Packet filters*: These filter traffic coming into and going out of a network.
- *Proxy server*: A proxy server captures all requests to the real server and tries to process the request made by the user.
- *Authentication system*: This authenticates users based on usernames and passwords.
- **Network address translation (NAT) software**: This type of software separates IP addresses into two sets, enabling LANs to use the addresses for internal and external traffic.

## Firewall Configuration

Firewalls are complex things to configure. Before the firewall is installed, the administrator should be familiar with the features and operation of the firewall. Its operation can be understood using the manual, documentation, knowledge base entries, and technical support. Firewalls should be configured and administered by experienced people, as firewall logs can be used in court as evidence. The following firewall functions should be addressed during the configuration process:

- *Proxies*: Proxies should be used to limit traffic to the designated protocols. Proxies are able to block file-sharing programs such as Kazaa and iMesh and can even defeat hacking tools.
- *Comments*: Comment entries can be included in packet filters. Firewall rules can change often, and it is important to know the reasoning behind every rule.
- *Grouping*: Grouping is the process of arranging computers with the same security requirements. The complexity of the firewall rules and the potential for human error can be reduced and minimized with the help of grouping.
- *Accounts*: The creation of an individual account for every administrator will make the firewall easier to maintain.
- *Configuration tracking*: Configuration tracking helps administrators determine the differences between the older configuration and the current configuration. This is useful in case something is wrong with the current configuration.
- *NAT*: On each external interface, the administrator should enable network address translation. NAT changes the internal IP address of a workstation to the external IP of the firewall. The outside world sees only the external address.
- *Passwords*: Passwords should be alphanumeric and configured to expire in three months.
- *Logs*: The administrator should schedule the binary logs to be exported to an FTP server. The system logs should be copied to the central log server. Log management should be configured to prevent consumption of the system disk.
- *Alerts*: The firewall should send alerts when it encounters any suspicious events. Notification methods include alert windows, e-mail, pager, SMS, and syslog.

## Software Firewall

**Software firewalls** are pieces of software that sit between user applications and the networking components of the operating system. A software firewall implants itself in a key area of the application/network path, and it analyzes traffic against its rule set. Anything that follows the allowed rules is permitted to pass, and anything that does not is dropped. There are two main areas that a software firewall focuses on: the actual packet level and the individual process level.

### *Actual Packet Level*

The responsibility at the actual packet level is to look for suspicious or malformed packets, detect port scans, and assess whether or not packets are allowed to pass to the protocol stack. Packets are evaluated against networking criteria such as the formal validity of the packet, direction of the packet, destination host and port, and packet flags.

### Individual Process Level

This component works at a higher level, and it deals with individual processes. It checks whether a process is allowed to initiate a connection to a given host on a given port or whether it is allowed to listen on a given port.

## Hardware Firewall

A *hardware firewall* is a dedicated device that is meant only for firewalling. A hardware firewall performs routing and additional functions. This type of firewall handles large amounts of network traffic and is placed on the perimeter of the network to filter Internet noise and allow only allowed traffic into the network.

## Types of Firewalls

### IP Packet-Filter Firewall

An IP packet-filter firewall creates its own set of rules to either discard or accept traffic over a network connection, as shown in Figure 2-1. When the packet filter receives the packet, it compares it to the set of rules. Packet filters typically permit or deny network traffic based on the following factors:

- The addresses of both the source and destination
- Protocols such as TCP, UDP, or ICMP
- Source and destination ports, and ICMP types and codes
- Flags in the TCP header, if the packet is a connect request
- Direction of the packet
- Which physical interface the packet is traversing

Commonly, IP packet filters are stateless. This means that the packet filter doesn't remember any packets that were previously processed. A stateful packet filter is able to store information about previous traffic. Stateless packet filters are more vulnerable to spoofing, as intruders can easily forge the source IP address and the acknowledgment bit in the IP packet header.

### Circuit-Level Gateway

A circuit-level gateway operates at the session layer of the OSI model, as shown in Figure 2-2. It analyzes the TCP handshaking process to determine whether a particular session is legitimate. The information generated from the circuit-level gateway appears to be created or originated from the gateway. It is useful for hiding information about protected networks. These types of firewalls are comparatively inexpensive. One disadvantage of these types of firewalls is that they do not filter individual packets.

| IP filter rules | IP filter values |
|---|---|
| UDP inbound traffic filter rule | Allow port 4500 for VPN gateway addresses |
| UDP inbound traffic filter rule | Allow port 500 for VPN gateway addresses |
| UDP outbound traffic filter rule | Allow port 4500 for VPN gateway IP addresses |
| UDP outbound traffic filter rule | Allow port 500 for VPN gateway IP addresses |
| ESP inbound traffic filter rule | Allow ESP protocol (X'32') for VPN gateway IP addresses |
| ESP outbound traffic filter rule | Allow ESP protocol (X'32') for VPN gateway IP addresses |

**Figure 2-1**    An IP packet-filter firewall contains a set of rules regarding acceptable network traffic.

## Application-Level Gateway

Application-level gateways are also known as proxies. Their functions are similar to circuit-level gateways, except that they are application specific and are able to filter traffic at the application layer of the OSI model, as shown in Figure 2-3. Application-level gateways can also log user activity and logins.

## Network-Level Firewalls

The first generation of firewalls operates at the network level. These firewalls inspect the packet header and filter traffic based on the IP address of the source, the destination port, and the requested service. Sometimes, filtration is done based on protocols or domain name of the source. These firewalls, by default, are built into network devices such as routers. They do not support rule-based models and cannot understand HTML or XML.

*PIX Firewall*  PIX firewalls run on proprietary embedded operating systems. The firewall is a dedicated system that has a single main function.

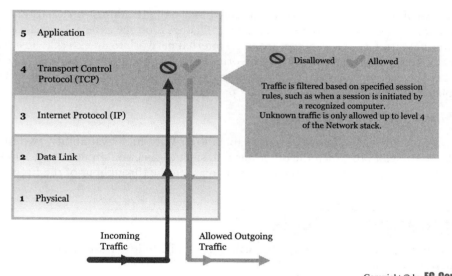

**Figure 2-2**  Circuit-level gateways operate at the session layer of the OSI model.

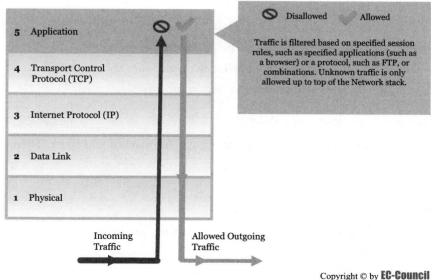

**Figure 2-3**  Application level gateways function at the application layer of the OSI model.

## Firewall Features

Most organizations need more than what a firewall can offer. An administrator should check for the following features when choosing a firewall for an organization:

- Preference of a software firewall that can be installed on a new or existing PC or a dedicated machine
- Number of firewall sessions the firewall can support
- Number of VPN protocols that are viewable
- Ability to communicate with Exchange mail server or SharePoint collaboration server
- Preferred type of management interface, e.g., command-line interface (CLI), graphical management console, or Web-based interface

Many firewalls come with features such as NAT, high availability, and failover.

### Network Address Translation (NAT)

*Network address translation (NAT)* is a process used to change the IP address on a packet to a different IP address relevant to another network. A router has a single IP address on the external interface and a nonroutable address on the internal interface. Packets sent from the internal network to an external host have a single IP address, and it appears to the host that the packets are originating from a single IP address. The hiding of internal IP addresses makes the task more difficult for traffic analysis and launching of denial-of-service (DoS) attacks. NAT can be applied to both incoming and outgoing packets.

### High Availability and Failover

Some high-end firewalls provide high-availability capabilities. With high availability, two firewalls can run simultaneously. If one firewall fails, then the other one will start to function immediately. Some high-availability solutions provide clustering capabilities, enabling an increase in the throughput of the firewall.

# Firewall Configuration Strategies

There are several strategies for configuring a firewall. Steps to be followed for firewall configuration in an organization are described following.

## How to Choose a Firewall

When choosing a firewall for organizations, certain questions must be answered, such as the following:

- Why is the firewall being implemented?
- How will the firewall fit into the topology?
- What form of traffic inspection is going to be performed?
- Is the organization compatible with the appliance or software solution?
- What operating system is best suited for that environment?

### Selecting the Right Firewall Topology

The most important task is to place the firewall where it will have maximum effect. There are three basic options:

1. Bastion host
2. Screened subnet
3. Dual firewalls

Once a topology that best suits the IT infrastructure of the organization is determined, the next step is to place the individual system in that topology.

## Scalability

The scalability of a firewall is calculated from the performance statistics of the device. Scalability can be achieved through vertical scaling (scaling up) or horizontal scaling (scaling out).

### Vertical Scaling (Scaling Up)

Variation in the degree of scalability can be achieved by increasing the memory, processing power of the CPU, or throughput of the network interfaces. This type of scalability variation does not depend on whether the firewall is hardware or software.

### Horizontal Scaling (Scaling Out)

Most firewalls have the ability to scale out with the help of load balancing. Multiple servers are arranged in a cluster and are viewed as a single server from the client side. Some hardware firewalls are designed specifically with scaling out in mind, as the devices can be stacked to operate as a single load-balancing unit.

## Firewall Architecture

### Dual-Homed Host Architecture

Dual-homed architecture is built around a dual-homed host computer, as shown in Figure 2-4. A dual-homed host computer is a computer with at least two interfaces. These types of hosts have the ability to route the IP packets from one network to another. Systems behind the firewall can communicate with the dual-homed host. Those systems that are outside the firewall communicate only with the dual-homed host and cannot communicate directly with the systems behind the firewall. Services that dual-homed hosts provide are through proxies.

### Screened Host Architecture

The services that a screened host architecture provides are from a host that is connected to the internal network and is using a separate router, as shown in Figure 2-5. Packet filtering provides the primary security in this architecture.

In the internal network, there is a bastion host. By setting the packet filter in the screening router, the screened host can open a connection to the bastion host. The bastion host requires a high level of security.

The configuration of the packet filtering in the router is performed to enable the following:

- Opening connections to hosts on the Internet for certain services
- Disallowing all connections from the internal hosts

### Screened Subnet Architecture

In this architecture, an extra layer of security can be added by adding a perimeter network, which can isolate the internal network from the Internet, as shown in Figure 2-6. The bastion hosts are the machines that are most

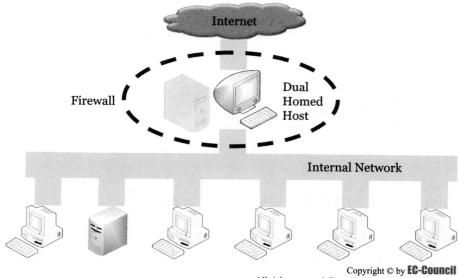

**Figure 2-4**  Dual-homed architecture is built around a dual-homed host computer.

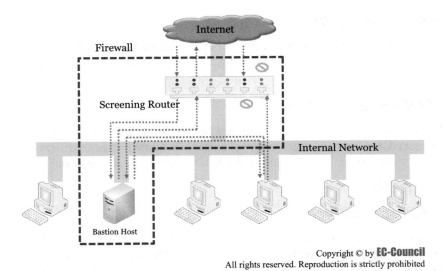

**Figure 2-5** Screened host architecture provides services through a host that uses a separate router.

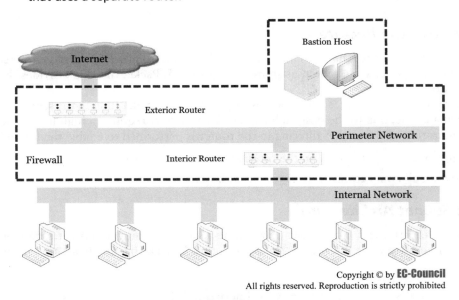

**Figure 2-6** In a screened subnet architecture, the bastion hosts are isolated on a perimeter network.

frequently attacked. In a screened subnet architecture, the bastion hosts are isolated on a perimeter network. Thus, the impact of an attack on a bastion host can be minimized.

The simplest type of screened subnet architecture involves two screening routers connected to a perimeter network. One is placed between the perimeter network and the internal network, and the other is placed between the perimeter network and the external network. If an intruder is trying to break this type of architecture, then the intruder has to break these two routers.

# Securing Against Hacking by Using a Firewall

## Handling Threats and Security Tasks

### *Restricting Access from Outside the Network*

Restricting unnecessary data access is the primary focus of any firewall. The firewall observes each data packet for the presence of authorized protocols and IP addresses in an approved list. It also performs packet filtering to handle a potential attack by scanning for network addresses and open ports. Initially, a hacker may use special software to scan IP addresses and ports while connecting to a network; if there is a response from a computer, the hacker targets that computer. A hacker performs a port scan to identify what services are available. Open, unused ports are vulnerabilities that firewalls must be aware of. A firewall blocks certain services to prevent outsiders from accessing services such as print and file sharing through an open port.

To find the number of connections that are open on a Windows-based computer, an administrator should run **netstat -an** at a command prompt. This command displays all open connections and listening ports on the computer.

### Restricting Access from Inside the Network

It is difficult to secure a network from internal attacks. To protect the network from those types of threats in the organization, the following preventive measures should be taken:

1. Disallow users from inserting virus-infected floppy disks into the system.
2. Restrict employees from using remote access software from home that bypasses the perimeter firewall.
3. Educate employees about social engineering, an attack in which hackers gather confidential information by interacting with employees to collect passwords, IP addresses, server names, and other information about the network.

### Restricting Client Access to External Hosts

Firewalls not only restrict unauthorized traffic from entering the network from outside, they also disallow traffic from inside the network to the outside Internet. They can act as a proxy server that allows high-level application connections related to internal hosts and other machines. A single firewall can provide both outbound packet filtering and proxy services. Application proxies restrict the user from gaining unrestricted access to the Internet, although some technically sophisticated users might be able to circumvent the security systems. The user might dial through a remote access program and open a security hole. Remote access programs, such as GoToMyPC, are used to access client software installed on home and work computers. This software is configured so that every 15 or 20 seconds, the computer sends the query "Does anyone want to connect?" The firewall may not check for such traffic, presenting a security risk.

## Protection Against Hacking

Hacking is an attempt to infiltrate a computer or network to steal data, to cause harm, or possibly just to claim credit. A good example is to identify theft that results from a hacker attack on an individual. These attacks have the following potential impacts on large organizations:

- *Loss of data*: Many organizations use the Internet to process the payroll, health insurance information, and staff directories. If these data are lost, it may affect the organization.
- *Loss of time*: The time spent recovering files, rebuilding servers, and patching security breaches is detrimental to an organization's effectiveness.
- *Loss of staff resources*: Recovering from hacking attacks creates a large drain on personnel.

## Centralization and Documentation

### Providing Centralization

A firewall integrates security and thus aids in the security-related activities of the network administrator. A firewall placed on the perimeter of a network provides a single location for implementing border security policies and for monitoring traffic coming into and going out of the organization's network.

### Enabling Documentation

Each firewall must be configured so that it can provide data to network administrators in the form of log files. These log files record attempted breaches such as illegal file access, unauthorized connection attempts, and so on. Going through the log files is a complex task, but these files help an administrator recognize any compromises in the security system so that he or she can repair any problems. Another purpose of providing documentation is to allow an administrator to identify or track intruders so that they can be held in case any theft or damage occurs. Periodically auditing and analyzing log file data makes firewalls efficient, since methods of attack vary from time to time. Firewalls must be assessed and adjusted to report new viruses and threats.

## Multilayer Firewall Protection

The use of firewalls to protect networks from external attacks is a widely accepted function. The most complex strategy is an interior and exterior router in a network, a DMZ, and one or more bastion hosts within the DMZ. The following OSI layers are best protected by specific firewall technologies:

- Layer 7
  - OSI reference model: Application
  - Firewall technology: Application-level gateway
- Layer 6
  - OSI reference model: Presentation
  - Firewall technology: Encryption
- Layer 5
  - OSI reference model: Session
  - Firewall technology: SOCKS proxy server
- Layer 4
  - OSI reference model: Transport
  - Firewall technology: Packet filtering
- Layer 3
  - OSI reference model: Network
  - Firewall technology: NAT
- Layer 2
  - OSI reference model: Data link
  - Firewall technology: N/A
- Layer 1
  - OSI reference model: Physical
  - Firewall technology: N/A

# Understanding the Concept of DMZs

A *DMZ (demilitarized zone)* resides outside an internal network and offers open access to servers such as Web servers and host-and-router setups. A host-and-router setup is an arrangement in which the host consists of a router that directs traffic flow to itself and other machines.

## Firewall Deployment Strategies

### Screened Host

A screened host has functions similar to a dual-homed gateway and bastion host; therefore, in some situations, it is called by both of these names. It requires two network connections using two interfaces, and it resides on the network perimeter but not behind the firewall. A router can be placed between the screened host and the Internet to perform packet filtering.

### Two Routers with One Firewall

In this configuration, the two routers are located on both sides of the screened host and act as a firewall. The external router is able to perform initial and static packet filtering. The internal router routes the traffic to its destination computers in the secured LAN. It can also perform stateful packet filtering to minimize the need for adding another router for this purpose. This type of setup is employed to provide in-depth defense for organizations such as the government and financial institutions.

## DMZ Screened Subnet

A DMZ screened subnet is built through the addition of servers that allow access to public services, such as the Web or FTP, to the subnet of the firewall, as shown in Figure 2-7. This setup is used when public access to servers such as Web and FTP servers is needed. The firewall within the DMZ screened subnet setup is also known as a three-pronged or tri-homed firewall. It is connected to three distinct networks and needs a separate NIC for each network. The following are the three networks:

1. The external network (the Internet or branch office)
2. The DMZ screened subnet
3. The secured LAN

The subnet within the DMZ, which is attached to the firewall, is also known as the service network or perimeter network. The service network contents vary depending on the company's specifications.

Three-pronged networks using a single firewall have the following advantages and disadvantages:

- The firewall needs only one set of configuration rules.
- To control traffic in both directions, the rules must be complicated.
- The license for a single firewall is less expensive than for two or more.
- The speed of the data flow decreases. As all the traffic has to pass through one firewall, bottlenecks can arise.

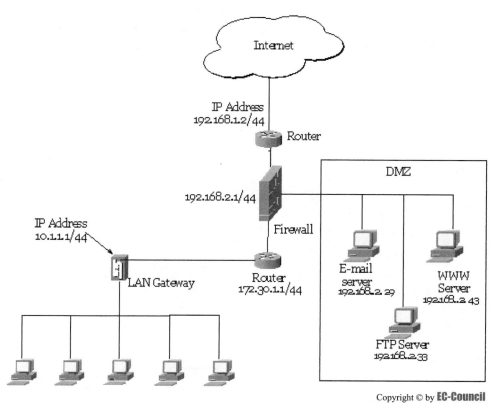

**Figure 2-7**   A DMZ screened subnet is used when public services such as the Web or FTP are being used.

## Multiple-Firewall DMZ

The services of protected networks are often made available for public Internet access. The firewalls that provide security to these networks are, consequently, very important. Large organizations install more than a single firewall to enhance security. The use of firewalls between the LANs and the Internet is mandatory for security reasons. However, the increase in security measures decreases the speed of the network and leads to performance degradation. Additional firewall setup is necessary for business and financial networks, as they need to provide services to the public with maximum assurance. They need to both provide confidential information and secure that information in a publicly accessible environment.

Multiple firewalls solve this problem and provide in-depth security. Multiple-firewall setups can be implemented in the following two ways:

1. Two firewalls and one DMZ
2. Two firewalls and two DMZs

*Two Firewalls, One DMZ*   The arrangement of two firewalls in a single DMZ is known as a *tri-homed fire-wall*. This term also refers to a single firewall connecting three interfaces, namely the internal network that it secures, the service network, and the Internet. Figure 2-8 illustrates the configuration of multiple firewalls. The three-pronged network can be configured with a single DMZ and more than a single firewall for the following reasons:

- One firewall controls the traffic flow between the DMZ and the Internet, and the other regulates traffic flow between the secured LAN and the DMZ.
- The second firewall acts as a failover firewall. If the first fails, the second can be used as a backup and provide uninterrupted service to the enterprise network.

One advantage to this system is that the traffic in the three networks can be regulated. For example, protocols such as HTTP can be identified and permitted for outbound data transfer, while other protocols are permitted for inbound data transfer. However, working with more than one firewall raises issues such as support for NAT, Kerberos, IPSec, and other security features. Only specific traffic can pass through the DMZ from the Internet, and this traffic is controlled between the DMZ and the protected LAN.

*Two Firewalls, Two DMZs*   An increase in the number of firewalls increases the complexity but makes DMZ deployment flexible. This enables the organization to employ separate DMZs for different parts of the

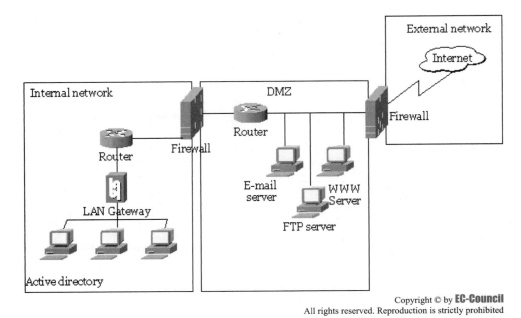

**Figure 2-8**   A three-pronged network can be configured with a single DMZ and more than one firewall.

network, which allows for load balancing. Figure 2-9 shows a firewall setup that includes two firewalls and two separate DMZs. The hub permits the external router to connect to the two firewalls and to have separate DMZs. One DMZ consists of public-accessible Web, e-mail, and FTP servers, while the other DMZ consists of a VPN tunnel server, which carries accounting files and other confidential information. Placing the tunnel server within the DMZ allows off-site workers who have tunneling client software installed on their systems to access servers in the secured LAN.

The two firewalls that are shown in the figure are both compatible models so that one can be used as a backup in case one of the firewalls fails. If the second one were not compatible, the entire network would stop working.

## Screening Router

*Screening routers* perform packet filtering between the client systems and the Internet, and are the simplest way of providing security. Screening routers can be installed in the subnet of a network, as shown in Figure 2-10. These routers function in the internal network and filter the traffic flowing through it.

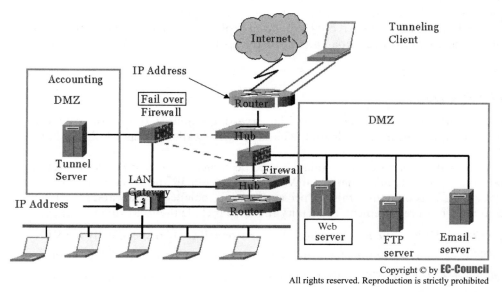

**Figure 2-9**  Multiple DMZs can be assigned to different parts of a network.

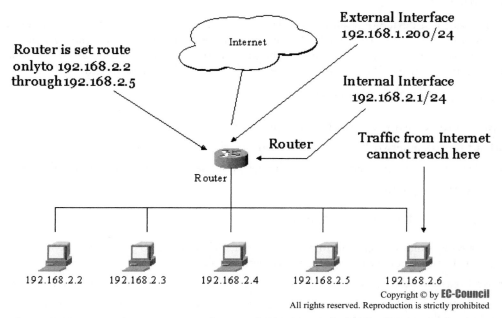

**Figure 2-10**  Screening routers can be installed in the subnet of a network and secured by a firewall.

The external interface—which connects to the outside network—and internal interface—which connects to the internal network—are the two interfaces of the router. Their IP addresses are distinct. The basic function of routers is to forward packets from one network to another. They use an ACL (access control list) to define the path of the flow of data through the interfaces. This list determines the types of network traffic that are blocked.

Static packet filtering allows for the flow of data though systems that are not connected. Advanced forms of routers perform stateful packet filtering.

### Dual-Homed Host

A dual-homed host is a personal computer that connects to the network, with a firewall providing its security. It has two interfaces through two NICs that are installed in the PC. One of the cards is assigned to the Internet, and the other is assigned to the LAN. The user can set up the configuration to allow traffic from specified networks as required. This option permits the user to secure the PC or home network.

The dual-homed host has some limitations if PC problems weaken the security the firewall provides. The firewall has the ability to perform packet filtering, but it cannot resist password-cracking attempts. The passwords can be cracked, as there is only a single layer of protection between the firewall and the PC. By providing in-depth security in the firewall architecture, the probability of attacks from intruders can be decreased.

## Specialty Firewalls and Reverse Firewalls

### Specialty Firewalls

*Specialty firewalls* are built to secure specific network communications. For instance, in cases in which an organization requires secure e-mails and Web access, firewalls such as MailMarshal and WebMarshal can be installed.

The two firewalls supervise and regulate a specific content type that flows through the network. They can block malicious code and junk e-mail. MailMarshal opens e-mail and scans it for malicious code before sending it to the recipient. This obviously raises a privacy issue. To balance privacy and security, the firewalls should be designed to meet both requirements. Specialty firewalls include the following examples:

- *OpenReach VPN software*: A packet-filtering firewall created specifically for VPNs
- *VOISS Proxy Firewall (VF-1)*: Creates safe voice communication over the Internet
- *Speedware Autobahn*: Works well with systems that run Speedware business reporting and analysis software

### Reverse Firewall

A reverse firewall is a device that supervises data. The firewall identifies DDoS (distributed denial-of-service) attacks by monitoring traffic to identify if more packets are flowing through the network than the expected number. If an overload is identified, it alerts the administrator. This feature can also be incorporated into a hardware or software firewall to eliminate the expenses of an additional firewall.

## Advantages of Using Firewalls

- Firewalls protect against intrusions into private networks.
- With a firewall, a network administrator can restrict the access of users.
- Privileges can be assigned according to the needs or the position of an individual user.
- They are easy to configure.

## Disadvantages of Using Firewalls

- They provide a main target for an attack. If an attacker wants to gain access to a network and breaks the firewall, then all network resources are vulnerable.
- Firewalls can restrict users from accessing valuable services and sometimes the Internet as well.
- Firewalls are not able to protect against backdoor attacks and can encourage users to enter and leave via backdoors when service restrictions are tight.
- Bottleneck conditions could occur if all connections pass through the firewall.

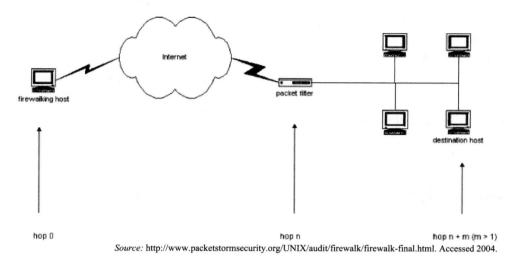

*Source:* http://www.packetstormsecurity.org/UNIX/audit/firewalk/firewalk-final.html. Accessed 2004.

**Figure 2-11**    Firewalking uses a technique similar to IP packet analysis.

- Firewalls are weak in protecting against smuggling, as users can send banned material or game programs through e-mail attachments.
- Firewalls do not always protect against insider attack.

## Threats

### *Firewalking*

Firewalking is a technique used to gather information about a remote network that has a firewall. It uses the same strategy as IP packet analysis, as shown in Figure 2-11. By using this process, an attacker can determine if a packet can pass from the attacker's host to the destination host through the firewall's packet filter. Before gathering information through the gateway response, the following two things are necessary:

1. The IP address of the last known gateway before the firewalking takes place
2. The IP address of the host located just behind the firewall.

### *Banner Grabbing*

Banner grabbing is a simple technique of connecting to a remote application and inspecting the output. Banner grabbing can also identify who created a service and its initiative. This technique works on standard ports such as HTTP port 80, SMTP port 25, and FTP port 21.

### *Placing Backdoors Through Firewalls*

If a hacker wants to continue accessing a penetrated system, installing a backdoor that cannot be easily detected will permit this. The type of backdoor needed depends on the firewall architecture used.

# Understanding Firewall Limitations

## Limitations of Firewalls

Firewalls themselves are capable of guarding a network and monitoring the traffic that passes through it. Firewalls can do two things: control access and protect protocol integrity. Some organizations do not allow direct connectivity to certain ports, or they may allow a secured connection.

Firewall limitations include the following issues:

- *Viruses*: There are many ways to encode a virus and transfer it over the Internet so that it can pass through a firewall undetected.
- *Physical attacks*: A firewall does not protect equipment; it can only block access to a network.

- *Architecture*: Implementing a single method of security or a single security mechanism has a single point of failure.
- *Configuration*: A firewall must be professionally configured.
- *Monitoring*: Firewalls do not have the ability to alert a network of an attack.
- *Masquerades*: A firewall cannot stop a hacker from stealing an employee's ID and password.
- *Policies*: Firewalls cannot replace strong security policies and manuals.
- *Vulnerabilities*: A firewall works on a given structure only and cannot recognize other vulnerabilities present in the network.

# Firewall Log Analysis

Firewall logs have a lot of information within them, such as the nature of the inbound and outbound traffic.

## Tool: Firewall Analyzer

Firewall Analyzer (Figure 2-12) is a browser-based firewall/VPN/proxy server reporting solution. Firewall Analyzer uses a built-in syslog server to store, analyze, and generate reports based on logs. These reports help the administrator secure the network from future threats.

Firewall Analyzer can provide the following information:

- Web sites visited by internal users
- Number of hits per server
- Amount of network activity originating on each side of the firewall
- Hacking attempts
- Origins of hacking attempts
- Real-time traffic monitoring
- Protocol usage
- VPN summary

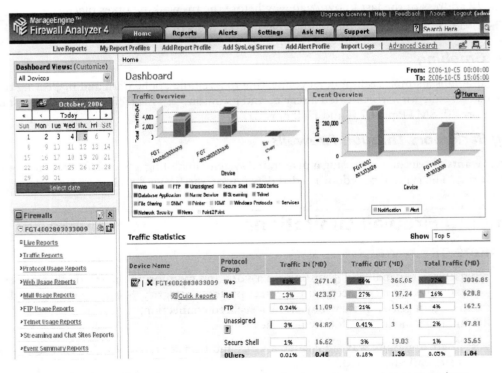

**Figure 2-12**   Firewall Analyzer uses a server to store, analyze, and report on logs.

Firewall Analyzer includes the following features and enhancements:

- Anomaly detection filters for network behavioral analysis
- User-based firewall views
- Firewall-based intranet settings
- Advanced searches
- Creating reports from search results
- Cisco PIX and Identiforce firewall administration reports for regulatory compliance
- Streaming and chat site reports
- Peer-to-peer attack reports
- Enhanced custom report profile creation
- HTML mail for alert profiles and anomaly profiles
- Provisions to test mail server settings
- Option for receiving reports in PDF instead of ZIP
- Rebranding of PDF reports
- Customizable number of records in scheduled PDF reports
- Quick reports for firewalls and Squid proxies
- Native syslog support for WatchGuard
- BlueCoat proxy log support
- Identiforce Gateway support
- Netfilter Linux IPTables support
- Snort syslog support
- NetCache log support
- Squid AWStats support

## Firewall Logs and Importing Logs

The Import Log File link allows an administrator to import a log file from a local machine or from a remote machine through FTP. The **Imported Log Files** page displays the list of log files imported, with details like the host from which it was imported and the status of the import.

*Importing a Log File*   The following are the steps for importing a log file:

1. Click the **Import Log File** link to import a new log file.
2. If the log file is on the local machine, choose **Local Host**. Click **Browse** to locate the log file.
3. The option **Ignore UnParsed/Junk Record**(s) enables Firewall Analyzer to skip those records in the imported log file that are in an unsupported format and to continue with parsing the subsequent supported records in the file. If not selected, Firewall Analyzer will not parse the entire log file even if one record is in an unsupported log format.
4. Click **Import** to import the log file into the database.
5. If the log file or an entire directory of log files is on a remote machine, choose **Remote Host**.
6. Enter the remote host's hostname or IP address, and the FTP username and password.
7. Enter the time interval after which Firewall Analyzer should retrieve new log files.
8. Enter the location on the remote machine where the log file or the entire directory containing the log files is present. Click the **List Remote Files/Directories** link to locate the file on the remote computer.
9. Click **Import** to import the log file into the database.

The supported formats for imported log files are shown below the **Location** box. If importing an unsupported log file, a warning message is shown.

### Firewall Log Archiving

Firewall Analyzer collects the logs from each device and archives the logs. These logs are then zipped at regular intervals.

### Loading Archive Files

The archive file page contains the files that have been zipped for each of the devices, including information about archive time, file size, and archiving status. To load the archived file into the database, a user can click the **Load into DB** link. After the file is loaded into the database, the user can search the archives.

### Viewing Data from Archived Files

Once the archive is fully loaded into the database, a user can click the **Report** link to search for specific data in the archive. In the pop-up window that opens, the user enters the criteria for the search, such as the firewall device, username, and protocol. A maximum of three criteria can be entered. The user then chooses the time interval that should be searched and clicks **Generate Report** to view the records that match the specified criteria.

# Firewall Tools

## Personal Firewall Software

### ZoneAlarm Pro

Zone Alarm Pro (Figure 2-13) protects a computer from hackers, spyware, and other Internet threats. It performs the following functions:

- Blocks unauthorized access to the computer
- Automatically makes the computer invisible on the Internet

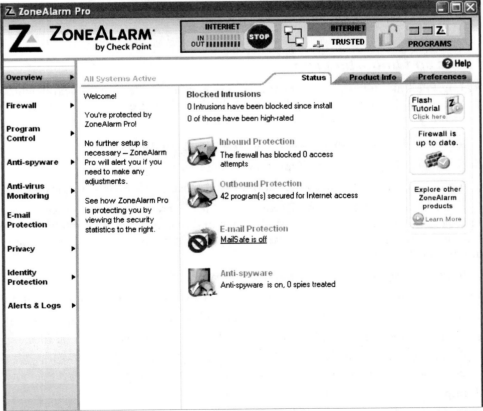

*Source:* http://www.zonealarm.com.au/main/zap_more_info.htm. Accessed 2004.

**Figure 2-13**   ZoneAlarm Pro is software that protects against hacking threats.

- Prevents spyware from sending personal information across the Internet
- Protects programs and operating systems from malware
- Automatically stops pop-up ads
- Quarantines suspicious attachments to help defend against unknown viruses
- Blocks users from accidentally visiting or being redirected to Web sites that distribute spyware
- Prevents spyware already on the computer from contacting Web sites to exchange information, give out personal data, or get updates

## Norton Internet Security

Norton Internet Security (Figure 2-14) automatically detects and blocks viruses, spyware, and worms. It has the following features:

- Advanced phishing protection identifies and blocks fraudulent Web sites.
- Rootkit protection finds and removes hidden threats in the operating system.
- Smart firewall blocks hackers and stops spyware from transmitting unauthorized information.
- Intrusion prevention automatically shields newly discovered security vulnerabilities.
- Full system scan performs a deep scan to remove existing viruses, spyware, and other threats.
- Norton Protection Center provides a central place to easily check overall security settings.

## McAfee Security Center

McAfee Security Center (Figure 2-15) has the following features:

- Automatically blocks, cleans, and removes viruses
- Blocks spyware before it is installed and removes existing spyware

**Figure 2-14**  Norton Internet Security protects against viruses, worms, and spyware.

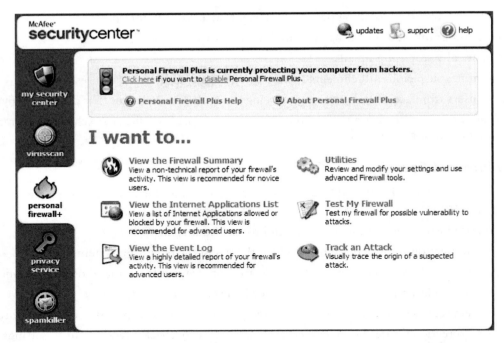

**Figure 2-15**    McAfee Personal Firewall provides protection from hacking attempts.

- Protects and conceals computers from hackers
- Improves PC performance
- Backs up and restores files
- Protects a user's online identity
- Prevents spam and e-mail scams
- Filters offensive content, pictures, and Web sites

### Windows Firewall

This firewall is a Windows component that has been included in Windows releases since Windows XP. The following are the steps to enable Windows Firewall:

1. Open Control Panel and then double-click **Windows Firewall**.
2. On the General tab, click **On (recommended)**, and then click **OK**.

The following steps should be taken to disable the Windows Firewall:

1. Open Control Panel and then double-click **Windows Firewall**.
2. On the General tab, click **Off (not recommended)**, and then click **OK**.

## Personal Firewall Hardware

### Linksys

Linksys makes routers that scan the data traveling over a peer-to-peer network. The Linksys firewall is also known as an Ethernet cable/DSL firewall router. The integrated SPI (stateful packet inspection) firewall blocks incoming or outgoing traffic. It also blocks inbound and outbound traffic at scheduled times and performs filtration by URL or keyword.

Typically, routers use NAT and basic port filtering to control the traffic through the router. By default, traffic coming from an external host is blocked by the router until it is specifically permitted. With the help of this restriction only, explicitly permitted traffic can access the protected hosts. The following are the three methods for explicitly permitting traffic:

- Port forwarding
- Port triggering
- DMZ forwarding

Linksys supports three methods of internal source filtering:

- By IP address
- By port range
- By MAC address

## NETGEAR

NETGEAR makes a rack-mountable SPI firewall. It supports up to 200 security associations (VPN tunnels). The FVX538 model can serve as a DHCP server, and it supports Simple Network Management Protocol (SNMP) and quality of service (QoS).

This VPN firewall extends security from the network core to the perimeter by preventing unauthorized network access using an SPI firewall, blocking DoS and other attacks, encrypting traffic traveling across the Internet, and adding support for antivirus and antispam policy enforcement, as shown in Figure 2-16.

The two WAN ports support two broadband connections. The second port is used when the primary broadband connection fails.

## Cisxo PIX

Cisco PIX (Figure 2-17) supports Simple Network Management Protocol (SNMP) traps. It has strong firewall security and proxy authentication functions, with NAT and PAT features. In a typical installation, the local port is connected to the internal network, and the outside port connects the Cisco PIX firewall to the DMZ segment. The configured Cisco PIX broadcasts a default route to the internal network and provides proxy Address Resolution Protocol (ARP) within the DMZ segment for the internal network hosts.

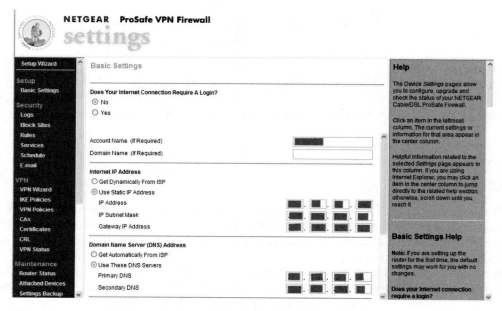

**Figure 2-16**   NETGEAR makes a rack-mountable firewall.

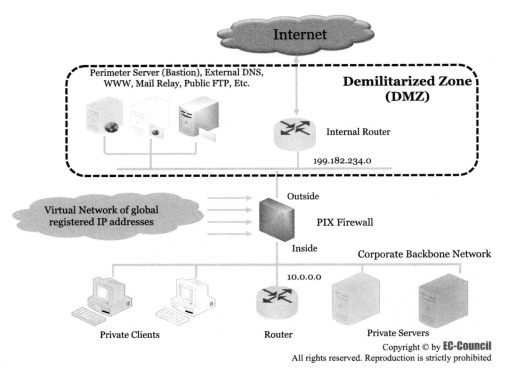

**Figure 2-17**    Cisco PIX firewalls use a virtual network of global registered IP addresses.

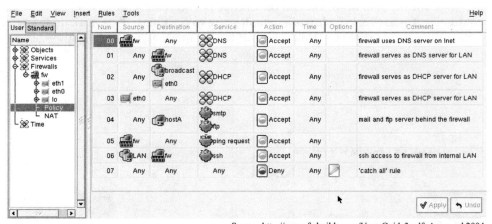

*Source:* http://www.fwbuilder.org/UsersGuide3.pdf. Accessed 2004.

**Figure 2-18**    Firewall Builder is a basic firewall configuration and management tool.

## Other Software Tools

### *Firewall Builder*

Firewall Builder (Figure 2-18) is a basic firewall configuration and management tool that runs on multiple platforms. It consists of a GUI and a set of policy compilers for various firewall platforms. Firewall Builder uses an object-oriented approach. A database of network objects is maintained and allows the user to edit policies using simple drag-and-drop operations.

The administrator works with an abstraction of firewall policy and NAT rules; software effectively hides specifics of a particular target firewall platform and helps the administrator focus on implementation of security policy. Back-end software components or policy compilers can deduce many parameters of policy rules using information available through network and service objects. They can then generate fairly complex code for the target firewall, thus relieving the administrator from having to remember all the firewall's details and limitations. Policy compilers can also run sanity checks on firewall rules and make sure typical errors are caught before a generated policy is deployed, as shown in Figure 2-19.

Firewall Builder includes the following features:

- More than 100 predefined objects for the most-used protocols and services
- The ability to create custom objects
- A network discovery tool that automatically creates multiple objects
- The ability to turn a firewall policy into a configuration file or a script file that can then be installed on the firewall
- Ability to print a single object firewall policy and export it in text or HTML format

### Wflogs

Wflogs is a firewall log analysis tool. It is used to produce a log summary report in text, HTML, or XML format, or to monitor firewall logs in real time. Wflogs is modular and relies on a library (libwflogs) that deals with the following input and output modules (static or shared):

- Input modules:
  - netfilter
  - ipchains
  - ipfilter
  - cisco_pix
  - cisco_ios
  - snort

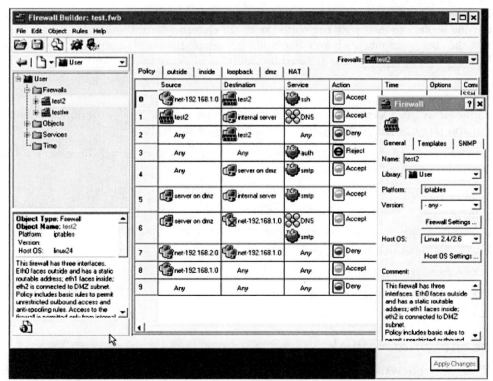

*Source:* http://www.fwbuilder.org/UsersGuide3.pdf. Accessed 2004.

**Figure 2-19**   Firewall Builder allows the user to run sanity checks.

- Output modules:
  - Summary: text, html, xml, human
  - Translation: netfilter, ipchains, ipfilter

The following are some examples of the ways Wflogs can be used:

- *wflogs -i netfilter -o html netfilter.log > logs.html*: Converts the given netfilter log file into an HTML report
- *wflogs --sort=protocol, -time -i netfilter -o text netfilter.log > logs.txt*: Converts the given netfilter log file into a sorted (by protocol number and then by reverse time) text report
- *wflogs -f '$start_time >= [this 3 days ago] && $start_time < [this 2 days ago] && $chainlabel =~ / (DROP|REJECT)/ && $sipaddr == 10.0.0.0/8 && $protocol == tcp && ($dport == ssh || $dport == telnet) && ($tcpflags & SYN)' -i netfilter -o text --summary=no*: Shows log entries (without summary) that match the given expression (refused connection attempts that occured 3 days ago to SSH and telnet ports coming from internal network 10.0.0.0/8)
- *wflogs -i netfilter -o text --resolve=0 --whois=0 netfilter.log*: Converts the given netfilter log file into a text report (default mode), disabling IP address reverse lookups and WHOIS lookups
- *wflogs -i netfilter -o xml netfilter.log > logs.xml*: Exports netfilter logs in XML
- *wflogs -i ipchains -o netfilter ipchains.log > netfilter.log*: Converts IPChains logs into netfilter log format
- *wflogs -i ipfilter -o human --datalen=yes ipfilter.log*: Produces a report about the ipfilter log file in natural language on stdout, displaying packet length (the **--datalen** option), which is not shown by default
- *wflogs -R -I*: Monitors logs in real time in an interactive shell

## Squid

Squid is a fully featured HTTP proxy. It offers a rich access control, authorization, and logging environment to develop Web-proxy and content-serving applications. Squid allows ISPs to save bandwidth through content caching. Cached content means that data are served locally, and users will see this through faster download speeds with frequently used content.

A well-tuned proxy server (even without caching) can improve user speeds purely by optimizing TCP flows. It is easy to tune servers to deal with the wide variety of elements found on the Internet.

Squid cuts the cost of coping with ever-demanding content growth. It also allows ISPs to prioritize and control certain Web content types where dictated by technical or economic reasons.

## Wingate

Wingate (Figure 2-20) is a sophisticated integrated Internet gateway and communications server designed to meet control and security needs. Wingate includes the following features:

- Provides secured and managed Internet access for entire networks via a single shared Internet connection or multiple shared Internet connections
- Enforces advanced and flexible access-control and acceptable-use policies
- Monitors usage in real time and maintains per-user and per-service audit logs
- Stops viruses, spam, and inappropriate content from entering the network
- Provides comprehensive Internet and intranet e-mail services
- Protects servers from internal or external threats
- Improves network performance and responsiveness with Web and DNS caching
- Eases administration burdens on internal networks

## Symantec Enterprise Firewall

Symantec Enterprise Firewall provides a secure connection with the Internet. It prevents the network from unwanted intrusion without slowing the traffic flow. It has a unique hybrid architecture that observes the information entering and leaving the organization's network. It provides high-speed connectivity between organizations.

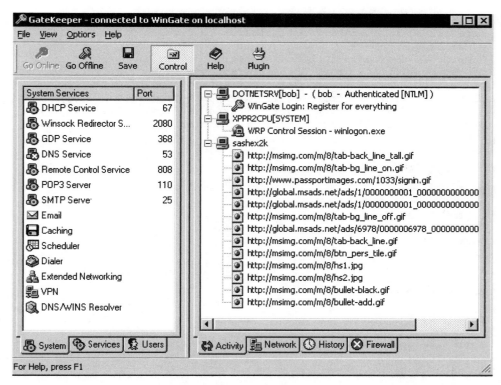

**Figure 2-20**    Wingate is an integrated Internet gateway and communications server.

Symantec Enterprise Firewall includes the following features:

- Supports the Advanced Encryption Standard (AES)
- Supports integrated load balancing that allows scalability to more than 1.5 Gbps
- Supports inbound and outbound NAT for both VPN and non-VPN traffic
- Supports URL filtering technology known as WebNOT, which controls the access to objectionable Web sites
- Integrates with proxy-secured, standards-based Symantec Enterprise VPN to provide secure and high-speed connectivity
- Simplifies policy configuration and management for any number of local and remote firewalls on several operating systems
- Produces log files consisting of information such as session duration, byte counts, complete URLs, usernames, and methods used for authentication

## Firewall Testers

### Firewalk

Firewalk is a network security tool that detects what the transport-layer protocols will pass. Firewalk sends TCP and UDP packets with a TTL field greater than the destination gateway. If the gateway allows the traffic, it forwards the packet to the next hop, where the packet will expire and elicit an ICMP_TIME_EXCEEDED message, as shown in Figure 2-21. If the response is received before the TTL is reached, the port is considered open; otherwise, the port is considered closed. It is significant to note the fact that the ultimate destination host does not have to be reached. It just needs to be somewhere downstream, on the other side of the gateway, from the scanning host.

```
zuul:#firewalk -n -P1-8 -pTCP 10.0.0.5 10.0.0.20
Firewalking through 10.0.0.5 (towards 10.0.0.20) with a maximum
of 25 hops.
Ramping up hopcounts to binding host...
probe:  1  TTL:  1  port 33434:  <response from> [10.0.0.1]
probe:  2  TTL:  2  port 33434:  <response from> [10.0.0.2]
probe:  3  TTL:  3  port 33434:  <response from> [10.0.0.3]
probe:  4  TTL:  4  port 33434:  <response from> [10.0.0.4]
probe:  5  TTL:  5  port 33434:  Bound scan: 5 hops <Gateway at
5 hops> [10.0.0.5]

port   1: open

port   2: open

port   3: open

port   4: open

port   5: open

port   6: open

port   7: *

port   8: open

13 packets sent, 12 replies received
```

**Figure 2-21**    Firewalk has the ability to determine open ports on a network.

### FTester

FTester is a tool designed for testing firewall filtering policies and intrusion detection system (IDS) capabilities. The tool consists of two Perl scripts, a packet injector (ftest), and the listening sniffer (ftestd). The first script injects custom packets, defined in ftest.conf, with a signature in the data part, while the sniffer listens for such marked packets. The scripts both write a log file in the same format. A difference between the two produced files (ftest.log and ftestd.log) shows the packets that were unable to reach the sniffer due to filtering rules if these two scripts are executed on hosts placed on two different sides of a firewall. A script called freport is also available for automatically parsing the log files.

# Chapter Summary

- A firewall is a program or machine placed at a network gateway server that helps protect a private network from users of a different network.

- A firewall provides perimeter security, because it functions on the outer boundary, or perimeter, of a network.

- An IP packet-filter firewall has a set of rules to either discard or accept traffic over a network connection.

- Network address translation (NAT) is used to change the IP address that is on a packet to a different IP address relevant to another network.

- Most firewalls have the ability to scale out with the help of load balancing.

- Dual-homed architecture is built around a dual-homed host computer, a computer with at least two interfaces that operate as a router between two networks.

- Firewalls not only restrict unauthorized traffic from entering the network from outside, they also disallow traffic from inside the network to the outside Internet.

- A DMZ (demilitarized zone) resides outside an internal network and offers open access to servers such as Web servers and host-and-router setups.

# Review Questions

1. What is a circuit-level gateway?

   _____

   _____

   _____

   _____

2. Describe the different types of firewall topologies.

   _____

   _____

   _____

   _____

3. Explain vertical and horizontal scaling.

   _____

   _____

   _____

   _____

4. Which architecture isolates the bastion host?

   _____

   _____

   _____

   _____

5. How can client access to external hosts be restricted?

   _____

   _____

   _____

   _____

6. What are the pros and cons of a three-pronged network?

   _____

   _____

   _____

   _____

7. What are the functions of a specialty firewall?

   _____

   _____

   _____

   _____

8. What are the functions of a reverse firewall?

_____

_____

_____

_____

9. What is firewalking?

_____

_____

_____

_____

10. What is the typical installation for Cisco PIX?

_____

_____

_____

_____

11. Describe the important functions of Wingate.

_____

_____

_____

_____

# Hands-On Projects

1. Navigate to Chapter 2 of the Student Resource Center and open Firewall and Proxy Server HOWTO.pdf. Read the following topics:

   ▪ Understanding Firewalls

   ▪ Firewall Architecture

2. Navigate to Chapter 2 of the Student Resource Center and open Why Do You Need a Firewall.pdf. Read the following topics:

   ▪ The Value of Your Network

   ▪ What Firewalls Do

# Chapter 3

# Packet Filtering and Proxy Servers

## Objectives

**After completing this chapter, you should be able to:**

- Understand packet filtering
- Understand the different types of packet filtering
- Enumerate the pros and cons of packet filtering
- Understand proxy servers
- Describe the authentication process in a proxy server
- Understand the security and benefits of a proxy server

## Key Terms

**Private IP addresses**   Internet Protocol addresses the Internet Assigned Numbers Authority (IANA) has reserved for private internets in one of the following three blocks: 10.0.0.0–10.255.255.255 (10/8 prefix), 172.16.0.0–172.31.255.255 (172.16/12 prefix), and 192.168.0.0–192.168.255.255 (192.168/16 prefix)

## Introduction to Packet Filtering and Proxy Servers

This chapter focuses on packet filtering and proxy servers. It first goes through the basics of and the different types of packet filtering. It then covers the pros and cons of packet filtering before moving on to a discussion of proxy servers.

## Understanding Packet Filtering

### Application-Layer Gateway

An application-layer gateway (ALG) operates in the application layer of the OSI network model. A proxy server is a type of ALG that acts as a protective layer for internal network applications by providing proxy services. Such services protect users from directly connecting to the Internet if any requests are made to access Web pages. Thus, viruses, worms, and other malware are prevented from infecting user computers. An ALG analyzes the contents that are requested and then decides whether to accept or reject the packets. It functions as an access control and controls internetworking issues. It also supports authentication and encryption.

### Work Process

Consider a scenario involving two users (A and B), where user A sends an HTTP request. The request first reaches the proxy server, which checks whether the transaction is valid and then encrypts the request. User B acknowledges by sending a response to A. The response is in the form of a MIME header and data. The gateway then checks for approval. If approved, the header and data are directed to the intended user, in this case, A.

### Network Address Translation (NAT)

Network address translation involves sharing a single globally routable IPv4 address, using multiple PCs on a private network. NAT is an IETF standard and is considered a transient solution for the IPv4 address exhaustion problem.

NAT offers packet filtering by transmitting only the requested traffic to private network hosts. The clients behind NAT have private IP addresses assigned by DHCP (Dynamic Host Configuration Protocol). *Private IP addresses* are Internet Protocol addresses the Internet Assigned Numbers Authority (IANA) has reserved for private internets in one of the following three blocks: 10.0.0.0–10.255.255.255 (10/8 prefix), 172.16.0.0–172.31.255.255 (172.16/12 prefix), and 192.168.0.0–192.168.255.255 (192.168/16 prefix). An application communicates with the server through a socket containing the source IP address, source port, destination IP address, destination port, and network protocol. Figure 3-1 depicts an example of NAT.

## Packet Filtering

Packet filtering monitors the data packets entering the network. It accepts only authorized data packets and rejects unauthorized data packets. It inspects the IP addresses, ports, and protocols of incoming and outgoing packets; determines whether to accept or reject each packet; and directs the packet to the intended location.

The following are a few sample packet-filtering rules:

- Outbound connections on HTTP, SMTP, and FTP are accepted
- Internet-related traffic can be accessed
- Data packets that hold features of IP header source routing are discarded

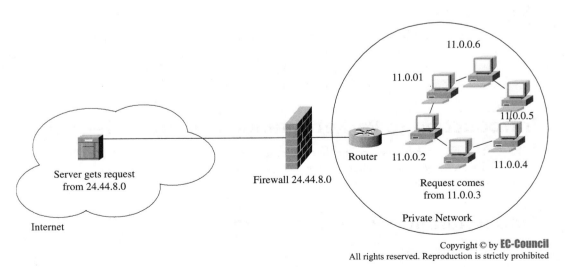

**Figure 3-1**  NAT allows multiple PCs to share a single globally routable IPv4 address.

# Packet Sequencing and Prioritization

## Packet Sequencing

When data are transmitted, they are split into smaller packets, with each packet having a sequence number. This process is called packet fragmentation (shown in Figure 3-2). The packets may not be received in the original order, so TCP/IP uses the sequence numbers to reorder the data packets on the receiving end. This is called packet sequencing.

*Packet-Fragmentation Attack* Through fragmentation, an attacker can manage to break through a firewall. The attacker sets the value of the fragment offset for the second packet so low that the second packet actually overwrites the data and part of the header of the first packet. If the first packet is accepted by the firewall, the firewall will see the fragment offset of the second packet and determine that the second packet is a fragment of another packet. The firewall won't check the second packet against its rule set, so an attacker can put data that the firewall usually blocks into the second packet. Since the second packet overwrote part of the first packet during reassembly, the attacker can use this technique to break through the firewall.

## Prioritization

The data packets sent from the host are entered into a queue and wait for processing. Packet prioritization is widely used and is a good technique for packet conditioning. Information in each packet specifies its priority. In Internet Protocol routers, scheduling algorithms decide which packets are serviced first. When congestion occurs, packet priority determines which packets are dropped.

## Scheduler

The scheduler decides which queues to process and in what order. A newly arrived packet is added to the end of the queue. If the queue is full, incoming packets are dropped. This is known as a tail drop.

There are two types of queuing:

1. Class-based queuing (CBQ)
2. Priority queuing

## Class-Based Queuing

This queuing algorithm divides the bandwidth of the network connection into multiple queues or classes. Traffic is assigned to a queue depending on the source or destination address, port number, and protocol. A queue can

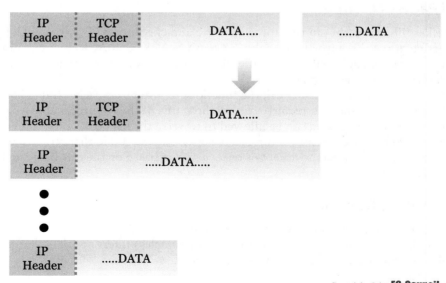

**Figure 3-2** The process of packet fragmentation splits a packet into smaller packets for transmission.

borrow bandwidth from the parent queue if the parent is underutilized. Queues also have assigned priorities, so a queue for SSH traffic can process its packets ahead of a queue containing FTP traffic. The class-based queuing system is arranged in hierarchical order. The root is at the top and defines the total bandwidth. The child queues are under the root queue, each having appropriate portions of the root queue. The following is an example queue list:

- Root queue (2 Mbps)
- Queue 1 (1 Mbps)
- Queue 2 (512 kbps)
- Queue 3 (512 kbps)

### Priority Queuing

Multiple queues are assigned to a network interface, with individual queues having a unique priority level. Higher-priority queues are processed before lower-priority queues. The structure of the priority queue is flat. The root queue defines the total bandwidth, and the subqueues are defined under the root. The following is an example queue list:

- Root queue (2 Mbps)
- Queue 1 (priority 1)
- Queue 2 (priority 2)
- Queue 3 (priority 3)

## Analyzing Packet Signatures

Signature analysis is based on the simple concept of string matching, also known as pattern matching. The incoming packets are matched byte by byte. The signature may contain a key phrase or command that is associated with an attack. If a packet's signature matches an attack string, an alert is generated.

# Configuring Filtering and Types of Filtering

## Types of Filtering

### Stateful Packet Filtering

Stateful packet filtering comes in two forms: generic and checkpoint. The tracking of TCP connections is performed starting at the three-way handshake (SYN, SYN/ACK, and ACK) and examines each TCP transaction in its entirety. Stateful packet filtering verifies whether a given transaction is valid or not based on the source and destination IP addresses and ports.

A stateful packet filter can perform all the functions of a stateless packet filter. The added feature of a stateful filter is that it can maintain a record defining the status of the connection. Based on the information in the packets, it decides which packets can be allowed to traverse the network.

A stateful packet filter contains both a rule base and a state table that records all active connections. The packet filter determines whether to accept or reject a packet based on the rule base and the state table. Figure 3-3 depicts stateful packet filtering.

### Stateless Packet Filtering

Stateless packet filtering determines whether to permit or block data transfers. It can completely block the transfer of data packets from the subnet to other networks. Stateless filters cost less than stateful filters.

The following are some of the criteria a stateless packet filter uses:

- IP header information
- TCP/UDP port number in use
- ICMP message type
- Fragmentation flags like ACK and SYN

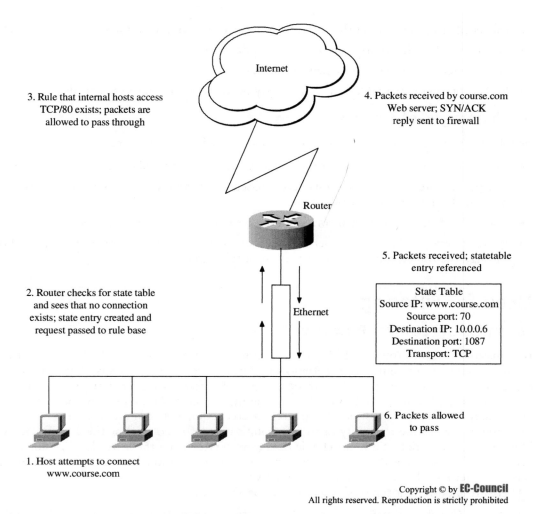

3. Rule that internal hosts access
TCP/80 exists; packets are
allowed to pass through

4. Packets received by course.com
Web server; SYN/ACK
reply sent to firewall

Router

5. Packets received; statetable
entry referenced

2. Router checks for state table
and sees that no connection
exists; state entry created and
request passed to rule base

Ethernet

State Table
Source IP: www.course.com
Source port: 70
Destination IP: 10.0.0.6
Destination port: 1087
Transport: TCP

6. Packets allowed
to pass

1. Host attempts to connect
www.course.com

**Figure 3-3**   Stateful packet filtering checks packets against a rule base and
a state table.

### Dynamic Packet Filtering

Dynamic packet filtering is similar to traditional packet filtering, but with some added features. Traditional filters are slower and very difficult to manage in a larger network that has complex security policies. Dynamic packet filtering is performed using information from the current packet, as well as the previous packet.

Filtering in a dynamic packet filter is based on the following:

- The IP address and ports allowed by the administrator at the network and transport layers
- The connection state
- The contents of the application layer

# Pros and Cons of Filtering

## Advantages of Filtering

The following are some of the advantages of packet filtering:

- Packet filters are relatively easy to install.
- The implementation of the packet filter security system is less complicated than other network security systems.
- The configuration of a packet filter is a relatively simple task.

- Packet filtering operates at the level of the network routers; thus, filtering is transparent to the end user.
- One packet-filtering router can protect an entire network.
- Simple packet filtering is extremely efficient.
- Packet filtering is available in a wide variety of software and hardware products.

## Disadvantages of Filtering

The following are some of the disadvantages associated with packet filtering:

- The connection is done from network to network, making the data susceptible to exposure.
- The packet filter denies and grants access based on destination and source ports. Authentication cannot be done through the packet filter.
- If a packet filter's rule set is incorrect, the filter will allow packets that it shouldn't.
- Packet filtering reduces router performance, as the packet filter examines every packet that passes through the router, thus increasing the time it takes to route them.

# Flags Used for Filtering

## Transmission Control Protocol (TCP)

Transmission Control Protocol (TCP) is intended for use as a highly reliable, host-to-host protocol in packet-switched computer communication networks and in interconnected systems of such networks. TCP is a connection oriented, end-to-end reliable protocol designed to fit into a layered hierarchy of protocols that support multinetwork applications. TCP provides reliable interprocess communication between pairs of processes in host computers attached to distinct, but interconnected, computer communication networks. Very few assumptions are made as to the reliability of the communication protocols below the TCP layer. TCP assumes it can obtain a simple and potentially unreliable datagram service from the lower-level protocols. In principle, TCP should be able to operate above a wide spectrum of communication systems, ranging from hardwired connections to packet-switched or circuit-switched networks.

There are six different types of flags used in the TCP header (shown in Figure 3-4):

1. *URG*: This flag identifies the incoming packet as urgent. If there is some problem with the data transfer and data processing is stopped, then the abort signal is sent with the URG pointer set so that the abort signal is processed first. If the URG pointer flag is set, the remote machine will not wait for the other fragments before processing the packet.

2. *ACK*: The acknowledgment flag signals the successful delivery of a packet. When a packet is received, the receiving machine sets the ACK flag and sends the packet to the sender. When the windowing technique is used, the receiver transmits an ACK only after a certain number of packets have been received.

3. *PSH*: PSH is the TCP push flag. Whenever a host sends data, those data are temporarily queued in the receiver's TCP buffer. This flag tells the receiver to immediately send all buffered data to the receiving application.

4. *RST*: The reset flag is used when a packet arrives at the host to establish a connection but there is no service on the host to handle such a request. The host rejects or discards the request packet and sends a reply with the RST flag set that indicates that the remote host has reset the connection. Hackers can use this feature of TCP to scan for open ports. The hacker constructs a valid packet with the SYN flag set and sends it to the target. If the target replies with an ACK with the RST flag set, then the attacker knows that port is not listening for connections. However, if the target replies with a regular ACK, the attacker knows that port is open and listening for connections.

5. *SYN*: The SYN flag is used to synchronize two hosts before the data transfer begins. The three-way handshake (Figure 3-5) requires that a SYN flag be initially sent to begin establishing a connection.

6. *FIN*: This flag indicates the end of the TCP session. It arrives after the last packet and helps tear down the connection. There is a possibility that until the other side also closes the connection, a host can still receive data after closing the connection. After the connection is closed on both sides, the buffer on either side is also released.

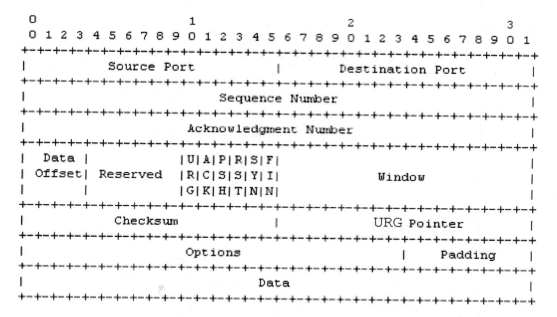

TCP Header Format

*Source:* http://asg.web.cmu.edu/rfc/rfc793.html. Accessed 2004.

**Figure 3-4**   There are six flags in the TCP header.

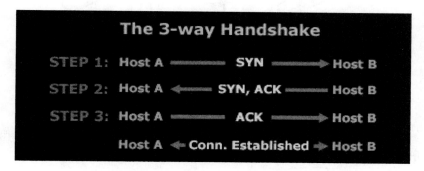

**Figure 3-5**   TCP uses a three-way handshake to establish a connection.

## User Datagram Protocol (UDP)

UDP is one of the transport protocols utilized in IP networks. It offers a limited amount of service and is an alternative to TCP. UDP is unreliable; it doesn't have error detection or correction. Even duplication of the datagram is not protected.

The UDP header, as shown in Figure 3-6, consists of 8 bytes of protocol information, with the following four 2-byte fields:

1. Source port

2. Destination port

3. UDP length

4. UDP checksum

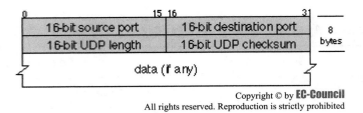

**Figure 3-6**   The UDP header contains four 2-byte fields.

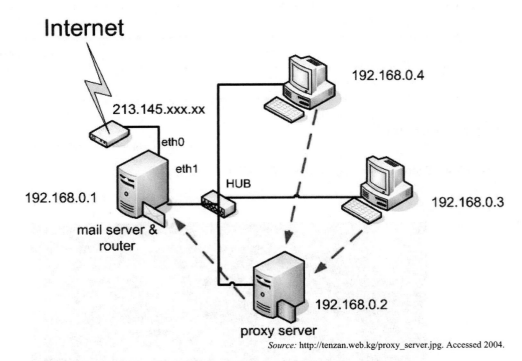

*Source:* http://tenzan.web.kg/proxy_server.jpg. Accessed 2004.

**Figure 3-7**   A proxy server hides and protects workstations from the outside network.

# Understanding Proxy Servers

A proxy server (Figure 3-7) works as a shield, protecting and hiding computers from the outside network. The proxy sends and receives encapsulated packets from specific applications. Web browsers and e-mail clients must be aware of a proxy on the network, as Internet access is typically funneled solely through the proxy when one is present. The proxy service listens for traffic on a particular port.

If there is a large group of users, network performance can be increased by using proxy servers. This is because information that users request can be cached in the proxy server, so the server doesn't have to access the remote site again to obtain information that has already been acquired and cached. An administrator can apply filtering to a proxy server to block access to certain Web sites.

## Role of Proxy Servers

A proxy server acts as a connecting link between internal users and an external host. It decides whether to obstruct or allow traffic based on rules provided by the proxy server administrator. The proxy server takes a request from an internal computer and sends it to the target computer on the Internet. The following describes how a proxy server functions:

1. An internal host requests access to a Web site.

2. The request goes through the proxy server. The proxy server examines the header and packet content and evaluates it against the rule base.

3. The proxy server reconstructs the data packet with a different source IP address.

4. The proxy server transmits the packet to the target address and conceals the actual end user who made the request.

5. Any reply that the target sends goes to the proxy server, which checks the reply packet against the rule base.

6. The proxy server reconstructs the reply packet and sends it to the source computer.

## Network Environment

The proxy server can share Internet access through the application level. Every individual client program can be configured to communicate with the proxy server. A proxy server is an effective way to limit Internet access. Firewalls also offer some of the same features as proxy servers, but this has not led to the elimination of proxy servers. The role of the proxy server is shifting from guard-dog security and connection sharing to the caching of contents and authentication.

In this day and age, the proxy server can also operate beyond the physical LAN. There is an increasing demand for portable authentication. For example, a university allows access to subscription-based third-party services. When students are not on campus, they can access the services through the proxy server, which in turn passes the authentication to the third party.

### Blocking and Unblocking URLs

URLs are blocked in order to prevent employees from visiting certain Web sites. URLs are represented either by IP addresses or DNS names. URL blocking is not entirely secure, since proxy servers generally block URLs as full-text URLs.

## Proxy Control

### Transparent Proxies

A transparent proxy is a proxy through which a client system connects without having to be configured to do so. Transparent proxies have some disadvantages; for example, it is not possible to automatically detect FTP or HTTPS connections.

### Nontransparent Proxies

A nontransparent proxy is a proxy that modifies requests and responses in order to provide some added service to the user agent, such as group annotation services, media-type transformation, protocol reduction, or anonymity filtering. Nontransparent proxy deployment is one in which the client is made aware of the proxy's existence.

### SOCKS Proxy

SOCKS is an IETF (Internet Engineering Task Force) standard. It is the generic proxy control for TCP/IP-based applications. It is like a proxy system that supports proxy-aware applications. The SOCKS proxy provides many Internet services, including HTTP, chat, and ICQ.

The SOCKS package contains the following components:

- A SOCKS server for the specified operating system
- A client program such as FTP, telnet, or an Internet browser
- A client library for SOCKS

The SOCKS server works on the application layer, and the SOCKS client works in between the application layer and the transport layer of the TCP/IP stack. For SOCKS proxy services, a TCP/IP protocol stack is used to access the SOCKS server, which then authenticates the request. The SOCKS proxy server doesn't allow external network components to collect any information about the client that generated the request.

# Authentication in a Proxy Server

## Authentication Process

Authentication ensures a user's identification. The process allows a user to access only the resources he or she is allowed to access, providing greater security. The authentication process requires at least one of the following from the user:

- Password
- Physical possession, like a smart card
- Physical identifying characteristics such as fingerprints, voice scans, or retinal scans

There are three main types of authentication:

1. Basic authentication
2. Challenge-response authentication
3. Centralized authentication services

### Basic Authentication

Basic authentication is the most common form of authentication. A server maintains a secure database of usernames and their passwords. If the submitted username matches the password, the user can access the requested resources.

### Challenge-Response Authentication

The authenticating firewall creates and sends a code to authenticate the user. In response, the user appends a secret PIN to the code. If the code and PIN match, the user gains access to the requested resources.

### Centralized Authentication Services

Centralized authentication services support the following authentication practices:

- *Authentication*: Process of user identification
- *Authorization*: Identifying the authenticated user and permitting him or her to access the resources
- *Auditing*: A database that lists the users who are authenticated and to what extent they are authorized

## Application Proxy Firewall

An application proxy firewall is software that serves the function of both a firewall and a proxy. It accepts requests from clients, checks the request, translates the destination address, and sends the request on to the server on behalf of the client. The following are the two different types of application proxy firewalls:

- In a dual-homed host, a proxy server consists of two interfaces; one is enabled to the Internet and the other to the internal network. It is connected between the internal LAN and the Internet. The internal network hosts do not have direct access to the Internet. Proxy servers request the data packets and send these packets from the Internet to the internal hosts.
- In a screened-homed host, proxy server software filters the traffic present on both sides of the host.

# Understanding the Security and Benefits of a Proxy Server

## Security and Access Control

To prevent unauthorized IP packets from entering the network, the administrator should disable IP forwarding. The following are the steps for disabling IP forwarding:

1. Click **Start,** point to **Settings,** and then click **Control Panel**
2. Double-click **Network**
3. On the **Protocols** tab, click **TCP/IP Protocol,** and then click **Properties**
4. On the **Routing** tab, click to clear the **Enable IP Forwarding** check box, and then click **OK**

| Proxy Server | Packet Filtering |
|---|---|
| Also known as an application proxy | Also known as screening |
| Scans entire data packets | Scans only packet headers |
| Unsolicited data packets are reconstructed by the server | Unsolicited data packets are discarded |
| Acts as a mediator between the Internet and the internal hosts | Resides in the kernel |
| Server failure ceases all network communication | Packet filter failure causes all packets to be redirected to the internal hosts |

**Table 3-1**  These are some of the differences between proxy servers and packet filtering

Running a Web proxy or Winsock proxy service with access controls disabled is considered insecure. Adding the external IP address to the local address table (LAT) exposes the entire internal network to Internet servers and clients.

A strict password policy should be implemented to secure the network. The passwords, especially administrator passwords, that are used on the network should be difficult to guess. Network administrators should limit the number of people who have administrative privileges, and users should have only the rights necessary to do their jobs.

On the client machines, the gateway and DNS references should be removed. This prevents the clients from bypassing the proxy server to access the Internet. If a network uses DHCP to hand out IP addresses, the administrator should remove the same references to prevent the DHCP server from accessing addresses outside the internal network.

## Reverse Proxies

A reverse proxy sits between a server, typically a Web server, and the Internet. When a connection comes in from the Internet, the proxy either handles the connection itself or passes it along to the Web server. This provides the following features:

- *Security*: The reverse proxy partially protects the Web server.
- *Load balancing*: The reverse proxy can be used to balance the load among the servers in a cluster of Web servers.
- *Caching*: The reverse proxy can cache static and dynamic content that the Web server provides, so the reverse proxy is able to handle cached requests without having to contact the Web server. This enhances the performance of the Web server.

## How Proxy Servers Differ from Packet Filtering

Table 3-1 shows how proxy servers and packet filtering differ.

# Chapter Summary

- An application-layer gateway (ALG) operates in the application layer of the OSI network model. A proxy server is a type of ALG that acts as a protective layer for internal network applications.
- NAT offers packet filtering by transmitting only the requested traffic to private network hosts.
- There are two types of packet queuing: class-based queuing and priority queuing.
- There are three types of packet filtering: stateful filtering, stateless filtering, and dynamic filtering.
- A proxy server works as a shield, protecting and hiding computers from the outside network.
- A transparent proxy is a proxy through which a client system connects without having to be configured to do so.
- A nontransparent proxy is a proxy that modifies requests and responses in order to provide some added service to the user agent.

# Review Questions

1. Describe class-based queuing.

_____

_____

_____

_____

2. What is the purpose of packet fragmentation?

_____

_____

_____

_____

3. Explain network address translation (NAT).

_____

_____

_____

_____

4. Explain the difference between stateful and stateless packet filtering.

_____

_____

_____

_____

5. Explain the advantages and disadvantages of packet filtering.

_____

_____

_____

_____

6. Explain the use of the URG, SYN, and FIN flags.

_____

_____

_____

_____

7. Explain the concept of a proxy server.

_____

_____

_____

_____

8. Explain the difference between a transparent proxy and a nontransparent proxy.

_____

_____

_____

_____

9. Explain basic authentication.

_____

_____

_____

_____

10. What are the three different practices supported by centralized authentication services?

_____

_____

_____

_____

11. Explain reverse proxies.

_____

_____

_____

_____

# Hands-On Projects

1. Navigate to Chapter 3 of the Student Resource Center and open Packet_filtering_firewall. pdf. Read the following topics:

   - Packet Filtering Firewall
   - Table 1: Criteria

2. Navigate to Chapter 3 of the Student Resource Center and open Dynamic Packet Filtering. pdf. Read the following topics:

   - Dynamic Packet Filtering (DPF)
   - Introduction
   - What about the Fact SPI Can Prevent Attacks?

3. Navigate to Chapter 3 of the Student Resource Center and open Firewall-HOWTO.pdf. Read the following topics:

   - Installing the TIS Proxy Server
   - The SOCKS Proxy Server

4. Navigate to Chapter 3 of the Student Resource Center and open OpenBSD Packet Filter.pdf. Read the following topics:

   ▪ Packet Filtering

   ▪ Configuration

   ▪ PF: Tables

   ▪ PF: Network Address Translation (NAT)

5. Navigate to Chapter 3 of the Student Resource Center and open tcp_filtering.pdf. Read the Real Stateful TCP Packet Filtering in IP Filter topic.

# Chapter 4

# Bastion Hosts and Honeypots

## Objectives

**After completing this chapter, you should be able to:**

- Build and deploy bastion hosts
- Build and deploy honeypots
- Categorize honeypots based on levels of interaction
- Build a honeynet

## Key Terms

**Honeywall**   a honeynet gateway

## Introduction to Bastion Hosts and Honeypots

Bastion hosts and honeypots provide added security to a network. Both are completely exposed to attacks and are usually placed in a demilitarized zone (DMZ). By their location, which almost invites outside intrusions, they protect the systems that are inside the security perimeter. This chapter will familiarize you with the basics of bastion, or hardened, hosts and honeypots, and will teach you how to deploy and configure them.

## Bastion Hosts

A bastion host acts as a gateway between an internal private network and the outside public network. It is placed on the unrestricted side of the demilitarized zone (DMZ), so it is completely exposed to an attack. All unnecessary services are disabled to minimize the chance of misuse, and all security patches and updates are applied to make it as secure as possible. A bastion host provides a single entry point for the Internet. It provides services such as Web site hosting, e-mail servers, DNS servers, and FTP servers, which by their nature must be accessible from the Internet. Figure 4-1 shows bastion hosts in a firewall.

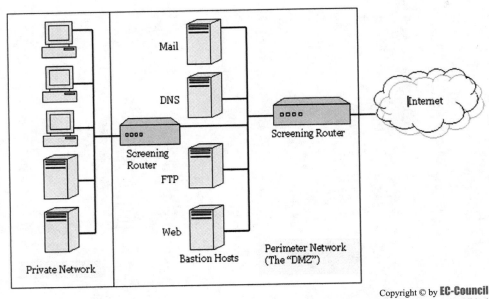

**Figure 4-1** Bastion hosts are placed between the private network and the Internet.

## Basics of a Bastion Host

A bastion host is a system that has multiple network interfaces exposed to the Internet. Because of this, its operating system is hardened to provide more security than usual. After configuring the system and installing the necessary software, the administrator can install and configure rule sets for internal and external traffic.

Bastion hosts create logs used by system administrators to find attacks and attack attempts. Two copies of these system logs are maintained as a backup. One way to back up the security logs is by connecting the bastion host to a dedicated computer whose sole function is to keep track of the secured backup logs.

The number of bastion hosts in a firewall is not restricted. Every bastion host can manage multiple Internet services on the same intranet. A bastion host can also be used as a victim machine, and can be used either to handle Internet services that the proxy cannot manage or Internet services whose security issues are unknown. The services are substituted with or added to other services on the victim machine instead of a bastion host. A victim machine can act as a backup to the bastion servers even if the server is down, but is generally placed in the DMZ as a possible target. It is a much tougher target than a honeypot would be, however it is still meant as a sacrificial unit.

If a filtering router is placed between the bastion host and the intranet, it will add further security. The filtering router drops all unauthorized packets between the Internet and the intranet.

A bastion host cannot manage a request, such as sending Web pages or delivering e-mail, when it directly receives that request; the request must be sent to the appropriate intranet server. The intranet server processes the request and then sends the reply to the bastion host. The bastion host then dispatches the requested service to the requester.

Bastion hosts run automated monitors, which are more complex programs than standard auditing software. They frequently check the bastion host's system logs and generate an alarm if any suspicious activities are found. For example, an alarm will be raised if it finds three unsuccessful logins in a row by the same user.

## Types of Bastion Hosts

The various types of bastion hosts have similar configurations, but each has different requirements.

### Nonrouting Dual-Homed Hosts

Nonrouting dual-homed hosts operate with multiple network connections, but the network connections don't interact with each other. One such host could be either the entire firewall or a component of a multifaceted firewall. If the host is a firewall, it should have predefined configurations.

### Victim Machines

When it is necessary to run services that are not secure and newer applications whose security flaws are not yet known, these services and applications can be installed on a victim machine. Such machines allow any user to log in. A victim machine should not run any other programs or services, to ensure there are no issues if it is compromised.

### Internal Bastion Hosts

In most configurations, the central bastion host is connected to certain internal hosts. For example, bastion hosts may pass an e-mail to an internal mail server, working with an internal name server. These internal servers are secondary bastion hosts, and they must be organized and handled like the primary bastion hosts. Very few services may be left enabled on these systems, but they must be configured in the same way the bastion hosts are configured.

### External Services Hosts

Bastion hosts are visible to everyone, which makes them vulnerable to attack. If one of the internal services provided to internal users is compromised, legitimate outsiders may not be able to use the services. If one of the pages of a Web site is replaced, everyone will be aware of the change. These machines should have more security features. They require only minimum access privileges to the internal network, providing only a few services.

### One-Box Firewalls

If a machine is constructed as a firewall, rather than as part of a firewall, it is prone to more attacks. The entire site's security relies on this single machine, so it is necessary to guarantee that this machine is absolutely secure. A replica of a system can be used to test any new configurations before implementing them.

## Building a Bastion Host

The following are the steps for building a bastion host:

1. Choose a machine to become the bastion host.
2. Disable all unnecessary services on this machine.
3. Install or modify the necessary services.
4. Reconfigure the machine to avoid any network vulnerabilities and execute operations as quickly as possible.
5. Establish baselines through a security audit.
6. Connect the machine to the network.

Make sure that the machine cannot access the Internet. Carefully document this process so that if the system or machine gets destroyed, it can be easily replaced.

### Requirements for Setting Up a Bastion Host

The following are some requirements for setting up a bastion host:

- Bastion hosts must be protected. All work done to set up the host must be properly documented.
- The required services must be installed and modified, and all unnecessary services must be removed.
- A secure audit will establish a baseline. The machine cannot access the Internet until the final step is reached and the bastion host is completely configured. If a firewall is to be added to a site that has a connection to the Internet, the bastion host must be configured as the standalone machine and should be isolated from the network.

If the bastion host is built when it is connected to the Internet, it might become an attack mechanism rather than a defense mechanism. Every possible precaution must be taken during the construction of the system.

*Hardware Requirements* A bastion host should have a consistent hardware design. The system and peripherals must be configured appropriately, and the configuration must be replaceable. Machines should have sufficient memory and processor speed. This does not require a fast CPU, however, it does require a machine that can monitor all the links or access points of the system concurrently. The machine is subject to the following requirements:

- It should be easy to add another disk to the system.
- All disks, including the boot disk, must be easy to attach and remove.
- Do not put applications with extensive graphical interfaces on the bastion host. This might encourage people to install more programs than is necessary.
- Bastion hosts must have appropriate, easily available hardware.

## Selecting the Host Machine

The machine should have the following features:

- Reliability
- Supportability
- Configurability

*Memory Considerations* A bastion host requires a large amount of memory. It uses caching proxies, which use a large amount of space for caching and usually a large amount of space for swapping.

*Processing Speed* The processing speed of a bastion host does not need to be very high. Many users use machines ranging from 2–5 MIPS for a bastion host, which is more than sufficient for an average site.

*Operating System* A bastion host offers a wide range of services. The recommended operating system for a bastion host is UNIX. UNIX provides several tools for the creation of bastion hosts as well as software for auditing and development. It offers online documentation that helps describe the configurations of bastion hosts. However, the UNIX operating system takes more time to configure and requires frequent updates.

The other operating system commonly used in bastion hosts is Windows NT. The complexity of Windows NT is much higher than that of UNIX, making it preferable to use UNIX whenever possible.

## Locating the Bastion Host

Bastion hosts act as checkpoints for outsiders. They separate the organization's internal servers from the outside network. There are several considerations when positioning the host within the network, such as physical location and network location.

*Physical Location* Bastion hosts should be located in a place where suitable environmental conditions, including proper ventilation and air conditioning, are present. They should be provided with uninterruptible power supplies and protected from unauthorized physical access.

*Network Location* A bastion host must be installed either in a network that does not carry sensitive data, or in a separate network of its own, known as a demilitarized zone (DMZ). Ethernet and Token Ring network interface cards often work in promiscuous mode. In this mode, the card captures all packets that pass through it. It will not only collect the packets of a particular system, but also those from other network interfaces such as Fiber Distributed Data Interface (FDDI).

To solve this problem, the bastion host must not be placed at the center of the network, but rather, at the perimeter of the network. Remember, it is the first line of defense, like a moat around a castle. The perimeter network is an additional layer placed between the internal network and the Internet. It is separated from the internal network by a router or a bridge. Internal traffic can exit and access the Internet, but it is invisible to the perimeter network.

## Securing the Machine Itself

To secure a bastion host, install a secured operating system such as Windows NT or UNIX. When using Windows, it is important to enable automatic updates. Be sure to install only a single OS, in order to make it more difficult for attackers to compromise the system.

## Selecting Services

Services the bastion host provides are mainly used to access the Internet. These services can be explained by the diagram in Figure 4-2.

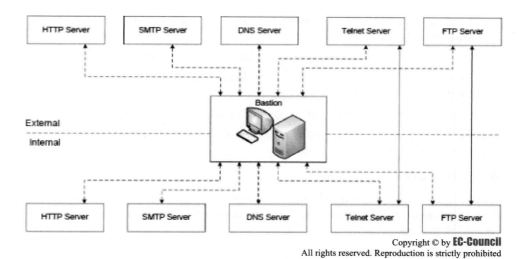

**Figure 4-2** The bastion host may run a variety of Internet services.

These services are divided into four parts, based on their level of security:

- Services that are secure
  - Services provided by the bastion host can be secured by using packet filtering.
- Services that are normally insecure but can be secured
- Services that are normally insecure and cannot be secured
  - These types of services are not recommended unless required.
- Services that are not used or are not used with the Internet
  - This type of service should be avoided and can be disabled.

Other important services provided by a bastion host include the following:

- Electronic mail (SMTP) is the most basic service provided by a host machine.
- FTP is used to transport files from one network/system to another.
- Gopher is used to retrieve information in a text/menu-based format.
- Wide-area information server (WAIS) is used as a client-server text searching system.
- HTTP
- Network News Transfer Protocol (NNTP) is used to provide information related to USENET news articles.

## Special Considerations for UNIX Systems

Most bastion host machines are UNIX based, but may also be Windows based. UNIX provides the following special features that should be considered:

- UNIX provides a user identification (uid) for single users as well as groups of users (gid). This identification is provided along with the users' respective login names. The main purpose of using uid and gid is to determine which files have been accessed by a specific user. The setuid command allows a user to run a program with the same rights as the owner of the program. The setgid command works similar to setuid, except that the user temporarily has the rights of the group.
- The chroot command allows a user to change the root directory for a running process. The process is no longer able to access files outside of its new root directory.

## Disabling Accounts

If possible, disable all user accounts on the bastion host. Reasons for disabling accounts include the following:

- User accounts can help attackers break into a bastion host. Attackers can hack the user accounts' passwords with the help of dictionary searches or brute-force searches, or they can capture the passwords using network eavesdropping techniques.

- User accounts reduce the reliability and stability of a system. Machines that do not use user accounts provide better stability.
- It is much more difficult to detect attacks when a user is using the system.
- In a bastion host, services like printing and local mail delivery are usually disabled. User accounts typically require those services.
- A user might create a security threat to a bastion host by using weak passwords.
- User accounts can be allowed on a bastion host only if the user monitors accounts and verifies them regularly to protect them from attackers.

### Disabling Unnecessary Services

Unnecessary files and applications should be deleted from the hard disk during setup. Only necessary services should be running on the bastion host. Any file, application, or service that is left could be identified by an intruder and then used to hack that system.

### Handling Backups

Backups in bastion hosts are quite tricky because of security issues. One way to handle backups is by using tape drives directly connected to bastion hosts. Backups should be done after removing devices from the network so that attackers cannot track the devices. Because a bastion host is a static machine, there is no need to have daily backups. A weekly or monthly backup is more than sufficient.

During backups, the administrator must protect the bastion host carefully. These backups mainly contain configuration details. An attacker who gains access to them can analyze the security of a bastion host without anyone's knowledge.

## Bastion Host Security Policy

Because bastion hosts are configured as standalone hosts, a group policy cannot be implemented. A bastion host security policy can be created using the following steps:

1. Install a new Windows Server 2003 and create a security policy with a new reference computer.
2. Install the Security Configuration Wizard component from the Windows Control Panel by clicking **Add/ Remove Programs** and then **Add/Remove Windows components.**
3. Install and configure the applications that will reside on the bastion host. This should include antivirus or antispyware software.
4. Launch the Security Configuration Wizard and create a new policy by pointing it to the reference computer.
5. Make sure that all the listed roles match the bastion host, and remove any roles that are not necessary.
6. Remove unnecessary client features, such as Microsoft networking client and DHCP client, in order to reduce server attacks.
7. Remove all administrative options except those that provide security to the system, such as firewalls.
8. Ensure that the additional required services have proper backup agents or antivirus protection.
9. Disable all unspecified services and test the configuration before it gets deployed on the network.
10. Import the policy settings from the INF file into the registry settings and audit policy settings.
11. Insert an appropriate security template and save the policy with an appropriate name, such as Bastion-Host.xml.
12. Test that application with a test server, and identify potential problems such as unnecessary services.

# Honeypots

A honeypot is a resource or tool that operates on the network. Honeypot security mechanisms are fundamentally different from other available security mechanisms in that, rather than repelling attacks, they invite them.

If a resource is perceived as having high value, it has a high chance of being attacked. Honeypots can prevent, detect, and respond to intruder activity based on how much interaction the intruder is having with the honeypot. Honeypots are not restricted to the single goal of keeping the network secured from a particular known attack, but are capable of performing a combination of various functions to achieve a large set of goals. They are capable of identifying unauthorized activities on a network in a manner similar to an IDS. They generate alarms by sensing automated attacks, viruses, and worms. They can also capture the activities of attackers through keystroke logging. The functions of a honeypot can vary based on its requirements.

## Types of Honeypots

Honeypots are classified into two types: production honeypots and research honeypots.

### Production Honeypots

Production honeypots are used to mitigate risk and divert hackers from probing and attacking production systems. They are widely used in securing systems and networks. Security can be categorized into three main parts: prevention, detection, and response.

*Prevention* Keeping systems or networks away from attackers is known as prevention. The best form of prevention is to apply authentication that allows access only to legitimate users. Encryption prevents attackers from reading or accessing private information like passwords or confidential documents. Encrypting the data in honeypots ensures that important information is kept confidential and is not accessed illicitly. Attackers waste time by attacking honeypots and are less likely to attempt to access the network in the future once they are aware of their presence in the organization.

*Detection* After an attacker has launched an attack on a network or system, it must be detected. The following are the main challenges for detection:

- False positives, where the system falsely sends alerts about suspicious or malicious activities
- False negatives, where the system fails to identify a valid attack
- When a large amount of data is collected, it can be difficult to aggregate and analyze all of the data

*Response* When an attack is detected, there must be a prompt response. Collecting evidence is necessary for both fixing the security breach and prosecuting the attacker.

### Research Honeypots

Research honeypots provide information on the attacker. Deploying honeypots across the company's network helps identify the strategies and tools attackers use. Research honeypots allow the attacker to attack and record his or her activities from the beginning to the end of the attack.

The advantages and uses of research honeypots include the following:

- They capture the automated attacks of worms and autorooters. The organization can immediately identify such threats and take measures to neutralize their effects.
- They help predict the probability of an attack. Honeypots deployed in various parts of the organization provide details for statistical modeling and reporting.
- They can capture tools and methods of attack that can be demonstrated as dtspcd attacks or covert NVP communication.

## Classifying Honeypots by Interaction

### Low-Interaction Honeypots

Low-interaction honeypots detect unauthorized access and system scans. They can be easily built, configured, deployed, and maintained. They allow less interaction with the attackers, thus reducing the risk factor.

Consider a UNIX server with services such as telnet and FTP. If an attacker uses telnet to attack, a banner with details about the operating system is shown. The attacker can attempt to break into the system using a brute-force technique or by randomly entering passwords. The honeypot captures these attempts.

Some known attacks are easily detected by installing a honeypot on the target system. The system administrator configures it to send alerts when it detects an attack. Low-interaction honeypots are easy to install and involve less risk. These honeypots, however, do not provide detailed information about the attacker, methods, and tools used for an attack.

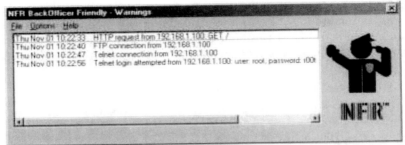

**Figure 4-3**  BackOfficer Friendly is designed to be simple to use.

Low-interaction honeypots provide minor details concerning attacks such as time and date, source and destination IP addresses, and ports used. Low-interaction honeypots are built to identify and record known patterns of attack. The honeypot's response to any given attack is predetermined.

*Honeyd* Honeyd is a freeware low-interaction honeypot for UNIX systems. Honeyd monitors the unused IP space, checking for connection attempts to those unused IP addresses. It intercepts those connections and interacts with the attacker by posing as a victim.

The user can also configure emulated services to monitor specific ports, like an emulated FTP server monitoring port 21 (TCP). When an attacker tries to connect to the emulated service, Honeyd detects and logs the activity, as well as all of the attacker's interactions. In the case of an emulated FTP server, it can trace the login and password of attackers and issue commands for tracing their activities. Almost all emulated services work in a similar manner.

If the attacker tries to act in a way that the emulation does not expect, Honeyd just generates an error message.

*BackOfficer Friendly* BackOfficer Friendly is a free low-interaction honeypot for Windows-based platforms. It helps protect telnet, FTP, SMTP, POP3, IMAP2, and other protocols by giving fake responses to hackers, wasting their time and resources. This tool (shown in Figure 4-3) can be used by anyone without prior technical knowledge.

*Specter* Specter is a commercial honeypot created by NetSec. It simulates a complete machine, providing common Internet services like SMTP, FTP, POP3, HTTP, and telnet. When the attacker connects to it, the honeypot generates an alert.

## Medium-Interaction Honeypots

These allow the attacker to advance, gathering details of the attack for analysis and reporting. There are several problems with this method, including the following:

- The added complexity makes it easier to misconfigure the honeypot.
- The virtual environment of the honeypot does not behave exactly like the real environment.
- Additional features cannot be easily added.
- It takes more time to install and configure.
- They can be very difficult to deploy compared to low-interaction honeypots.
- It is easier for the attacker to cause more damage to the system.

The advantage of a medium-interaction honeypot is that it captures more detailed information about the attacks, including information about the payloads, procedures, and tools used.

## High-Interaction Honeypots

Honeynets are examples of high-interaction honeypots. They are very complex and are difficult to build, deploy, and configure. The entire network can be attacked, but the architecture provides a controlled environment that secures the machine from being compromised. Within the network, victim machines are placed to misguide the attacker.

At the same time, the honeynet controls the attacker's activity using a honeywall gateway. This gateway permits inbound traffic to the victim systems and controls the outbound traffic using intrusion prevention technologies. The attacker gets the flexibility to interact with the victim systems, but no others.

The value of these honeypots depends on the extent of exploitation. The risk of damage should be properly handled. High-interaction honeypots are preferably located behind firewalls. Attackers that compromise this honeypot cannot use it as a tool to attack other systems. If the attacker is allowed to explore deep into the system, there is a high risk of damage, so firewalls and IDS need constant enhancement and monitoring.

Honeynets are discussed later in this chapter.

## Homemade Honeypots

A good knowledge of security tools, basic programming, and creativity are required to build a honeypot. The advantage of homemade honeypots is that they can be built to incorporate future changes. Homemade honeypots can be designed with simple or advanced features. They can create a virtual operating system to trap the attacker, and they range from low-interaction to high-interaction honeypots.

Most homemade honeypots are either port-monitoring honeypots or jailed honeypots. Port-monitoring honeypots listen to a port to identify any attacker's attempt to connect. They capture that connection and permit the hacker to interact with emulated services. They provide less interaction with the attacker, which means they acquire fewer details of the attack.

Jailed honeypots, also known as caged or chroot honeypots, are higher-interaction honeypots. The caged environment resides within the real operating system and includes a virtual operating system that imitates the real environment. This environment provides clear monitoring and control of the intruder's activities because the attacker will experience all the functionality of a real operating system. It provides a detailed report of the attack, unlike port-monitoring honeypots.

Other varieties of homemade honeypots are available, such as the one developed by Brad Spencer that identifies spammers and spam e-mails, and tiny honeypots like those built by George Bakos that permit attackers to hack in all possible ways.

### Port-Monitoring Honeypots

Port-monitoring honeypots are built to provide specific services, so they are restricted to certain functions. One method of building a honeypot involves an emulated service that allows the user to listen on a provided port. This creates an open socket that listens and logs the connections to it. The second method is to create an application that emulates certain services, including an intelligent response mechanism to the intruder's activities. If a connection from an attacker is identified, the honeypot sends the emulated data.

*Value* Port-monitoring honeypots are flexible. They excel in identifying scans, probes, and other unauthorized activity. They can listen to a number of ports on the network and can scan for malicious activities on those ports. This enhances the abilities of other varieties of honeypots.

Web services are commonly subjected to worm or autorooter attacks. The normal activity load on these servers makes it difficult to catch such attacks. Even an IDS can fail to provide the attack signature required to prevent such attacks. Honeypots identify such activity, generate alerts, and provide logs for review.

*Working* Security organizations can use port-monitoring honeypots to capture the payload and code of worms. Security mechanisms, such as an IDS or firewalls, can detect viruses but only a honeypot can capture the details and code of the worm to help the administrator analyze and research it.

*Risks* Port monitoring provides less interaction with the attacker. Because it limits the attacker's ability to damage the system, the risk is less. On the other hand, because the attacker is not allowed to interact with the real environment, there is less data to capture. If the platform is not secured, the attacker can still exploit the vulnerabilities of the honeypot's operating system.

### Jailed Honeypots

Jails are medium-interaction honeypots. They can collect more details than port-monitoring honeypots. They function by creating a virtual environment for the attacker that resembles the real operating system. They were designed for use as service mechanisms, to be accessed over risky networks such as the Internet. Services provided on the Internet are vulnerable to attacks, and attackers can compromise those services and use them as tools to attack others.

The principle of the jail is to confine the attacker to the services provided within the jail. The jail offers less functionality to keep the attacker from using it to attack other systems.

*Value* Jails are used both for research and production. They can monitor actions without the attacker's knowledge because attackers are attacking a virtual environment, consuming time and resources. Still, automated attacks cannot be deceived.

They provide details of an attack that can be used to analyze and research the tools, methods, and motives of the attacker. Jails can detect any kind of attack. Multiple applications need to be deployed to listen to all necessary ports. Complexity increases as the jail employs more applications.

*Risks* Jailed environments can track huge amounts of data. Jails do not imitate an operating system completely. Jailed environments were not originally built for honeypots, but were instead built as a safety device for companies who administer vulnerable services, such as a DNS or Web server. Jailed environments are very flexible and can be used for investigation. The disadvantage is that when a server like DNS is installed, the whole system is exposed to risk along with the individual DNS service. If the DNS service is weak, the hacker can take advantage of this and take control of the whole system. The hacker can compromise the operating system as well.

## ManTrap

ManTrap is a high-interaction honeypot created by Recourse Technologies. It functions using logically controlled virtual cages that provide the full functionality of an operating system. They can be attacked and compromised by an attacker, who believes the cage to be a real production system. This environment enables the administrator to capture the keystrokes of the attacker while the real operating system controls and monitors his or her activities. ManTrap can create up to four virtual cages on one physical system.

### Prevention

ManTrap can detect intruder activity by creating the feel of a real environment so that the attacker will believe it is real. However, if the attack is automated, such as by a worm or autoroot, it cannot be deceived or deterred. There are certain vulnerabilities in honeypots which can be compromised, but ManTrap is created to be more complex, which greatly consumes the attacker's time and resources to compromise it. While the intruder is trying to compromise the system, the administrator has enough time to react to the situation and stop the attack.

### Detection

Similar to other honeypots, ManTrap monitors the traffic flowing to and from the system, identifies attacks, and logs information. It has two specific methods for detection. The first is to listen to specific ports, detecting and interacting with attacks. The other is to scan the ports to which it is not listening. A passive sniffer detects the connections made to those ports.

ManTrap runs on real systems, which let the intruder penetrate as deep as possible, capturing more details of the attack. The vulnerabilities of RPC-based services that are exploited can be closely observed. When an attack is detected, ManTrap can redirect RPC-based traffic to other RPC-based services. The RPC network protocol has complex functionality. When these services are probed, ManTrap interacts with the attacker and captures the activities.

ManTrap detects attacks to other ports by capturing information at the network level, so that any attack on the 65,536 ports can be detected. The Sub7 Trojan and the W32/Leaves worm, which are both Windows based, scan port 27374 by default. ManTrap does not directly listen to that port, but it can detect attacks on this port with a passive sniffer.

### Response

Each cage in ManTrap appears to be a fully functional operating system. ManTrap captures the attacker's keystrokes, which provide critical information and help administrators make decisions on how to react to the attacks.

### Research

ManTrap has the ability to capture network-level activities such as known and unknown attacks, but its main value is in researching new attacks. Different cages can run different applications and discover all possible attacks on various applications. The ability to capture in-depth details of attacks, at both the system and network levels, increases its research value.

### Nontraditional Applications

ManTrap can test and validate the security tools and methods that an organization has adopted. The caged environment imitates production systems' functionality.

### Limitations

- ManTrap can only be used on the Solaris operating system.
- It is limited to applications supported by Solaris.
- It is limited to applications that can be executed in the caged environment.
- If RPC is enabled in one cage, it does not function in others.

## Advantages of Honeypots

### Valuable Data

Honeypots collect a large volume of data so that administrators can analyze the attacks. Honeypots reduce the noise level of data by only capturing high-value relevant data. If a connection to a honeypot is established, it means that an attack was definitely attempted. Honeypots scan the entire network for such attempts. The attacker may not always try to connect from the same system, but will instead use different IP addresses to pretend to be connecting from different systems. Such attacks cannot be identified by normal detection mechanisms and are considered to be attacks coming from totally different sources, but the honeypot identifies such attacks and records these critical data.

### Reduced False Positives

False positives on the network generate alarms and reduce the detection of real attacks. Honeypots possess the ability to identify only real attacks and unauthorized activities.

### Reduced False Negatives

Honeypots help trace and collect information on new attacks or behaviors.

### Low Resource Requirements

The major disadvantage of intrusion detection systems or firewalls is that they use a large amount of resources. All traffic needs to be scanned. The speed and size of the data does not permit an IDS to successfully monitor the entire network for malicious activities. Honeypots do not need to store large amounts of data or monitor all the packets flowing through the network. Honeypots check only the packets that target the honeypot and monitor only the activities directed at the honeypot. This significantly reduces the resource requirement. Any simple computer can be configured as a honeypot and placed on the network.

## Disadvantages of Honeypots

Honeypots cannot replace a traditional security mechanism because certain important requirements are not satisfied.

### Limited Field of View

Honeypots only detect the activities that are directed against them. Any other system can be attacked, and the honeypot will not notice it. The honeypot itself is vulnerable to attack from other systems on the network. If an attacker identifies the system on which a honeypot is installed, he or she can attack the rest of the network, and the honeypot will be unable to recognize what is happening.

### Fingerprinting

Fingerprinting is when an attacker identifies a honeypot due to its behavior. Subtle flaws reveal the presence of honeypots in an enterprise network. For instance, a honeypot could work like a Web server but might have a fingerprint in the form of a misspelled word in an HTML error message.

### Risk

Honeypots can be used as tools to attack other systems on the network if the attacker detects them.

## Legal Issues Related to Honeypots

The rules, regulations, and laws of using honeypots vary in different countries. Legal concerns include the need for data collection, the way the data are used, and the types of data collected. It is recommended that the legal concerns be addressed prior to the building and deploying of honeypots. Though U.S. law does not directly mention honeypot technology, there are three especially relevant statutes that should be examined:

- The Federal Wiretap Act (Title III) (18 USC §§ 2510–22)
- The Pen Register/Trap and Trace Statute (Pen/Trap) (18 USC §§ 3121–27)
- The Electronic Communication Privacy Act (ECPA) (18 USC §§ 2701–11)

### Privacy

Users are liable to lose small amounts of data unintentionally in any type of honeypot.

### Entrapment

A defendant can attempt to use entrapment as a defense to avoid conviction, but this applies only if a law enforcement official or an agent of law enforcement provokes someone to commit an offense for the purpose of consequent criminal prosecution when the defendant was not inclined to make the offense otherwise. However, this makes the assumption that the defendant wouldn't have otherwise made the attack. It also only applies to law enforcement agencies and their agents. Private organizations that are monitoring their own systems do not need to be concerned about entrapment. However, government organizations trying to detect fraud by deploying honeypots are at risk of the defendant using entrapment as a legal defense.

### Liability

If an unsecure honeypot is breached or compromised and used to attack another organization's systems, the honeypot operator can be held responsible. The responsibility of the legal counsel becomes tedious, as it becomes difficult to determine which state's law should be applied if the attack crosses state lines.

One safety measure that an organization can take to prevent this risk is to make it difficult for an intruder to use the honeypot's assets to exploit other systems. For low-interaction honeypots, the latest version of honeypot software and patches must be used. This guarantees that the honeypot software is secure and that the operating system is not in danger. For high-interaction honeypots, efficient data-control approaches must be used.

Honeypots can also be used to store and send illegal information, meaning the honeypot owner will be held responsible.

# Honeynets

High-interaction honeypots are called honeynets. Honeynets are deployed on production systems, such as a Web server. The following is the manner in which to deploy a honeynet:

- Create a network of standard production systems.
- Install security devices such as firewalls.
- Permit intruder activities. Services are not imitated and no jailed environment is provided.

The first honeynet was developed and published in August 1999. The Honeynet Project is a research group formed in June 2000 that investigated the strategies of attackers and their tools. They also defined the value of honeynets in their paper *Know Your Enemy*. The Honeynet Project formed the Honeynet Research Alliance in December 2001, which consists of organizations that research and deploy honeynets.

## Value of Honeynets

Honeynets are very flexible. They act as the following:

- Production systems that secure the company's network
- Research honeypots that provide in-depth details and methods of attacks

Different types of attacks can be identified for any specific system. Honeynets are designed to suit any type of operating system and have a very advanced responding mechanism. Using them as production systems makes their job complicated. They require a large amount of resources, consume more time, and are difficult to maintain. Still, they have great value as research systems.

Honeynets collect detailed information about keystrokes, conversations, and tools used to attack the systems. A step-by-step description of an attacker's activity is collected. This allows the honeynet to capture, analyze, and learn about previously unknown tools and strategies.

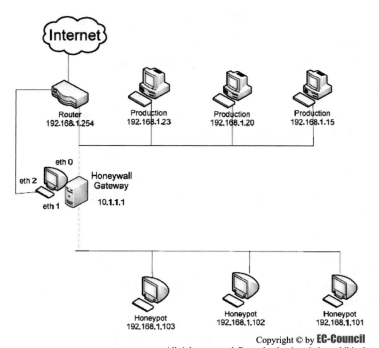

**Figure 4-4** A honeynet is a network of honeypots in a highly controlled network.

## Architecture of Honeynets

Honeynets receive probes, scans, and attacks. They work on behalf of a set of systems in the network, unlike honeypots that work on and for a single system. The honeynet architecture consists of a highly controlled network, like the one shown in Figure 4-4, in which any device or system can be placed. This architecture makes it easier to identify the attacker's activities, tools, and motives.

A honeynet's architecture is based on controlling, capturing, and collecting data.

### Controlling Data

A honeynet reduces risk and restricts the intruder's ability to influence systems outside the honeynet. Automating data control ensures quick reaction to attacks and also ensures that the attacker is unaware that his or her actions are being monitored and captured. Data control requires the following:

- Automated control requires human supervision for better results.
- A minimum of two layers of data control should be implemented in case one fails.
- The connection state of traffic should be monitored.
- Unauthorized activity should be handled within the required restrictions.
- System administrators should be able to assume data control at any point in time.
- Connections should be secured so that the intruder doesn't detect them.
- An alerting mechanism should be incorporated to warn administrators when a compromise is detected.

### Capturing Data

To effectively capture data, the following are required:

- Collected data should not be stored on the system that detects the attack.
- Any connections other than those of an intruder, such as when the administrator is testing tools, should not be stored in the logs.
- At the end of every year, system, application, and user activities must be archived.

- Administrators should have access to view captured data remotely.
- Data capture should be timed according to GMT.
- Data-capturing tools should be secured to maintain data integrity.

### Collecting Data

Organizations with multiple honeynets deployed in distributed environments need to aggregate the information collected by the honeynets. When collecting data:

- Use naming conventions to uniquely identify each honeynet.
- Maintain anonymous IP addresses to ensure confidentiality.
- To ensure synchronization of data available on multiple honeypots, time should be standardized using NTP.

## The Honeynet Project

The Honeynet Project is a voluntary nonprofit organization of security professionals established in April 1999. It is fully dedicated to providing help on security-related issues. It discusses topics such as the strategies of attackers, how they communicate, when they attack systems, and their actions after compromising the system. The Honeynet Project exists in the following four phases:

- *Phase I*: This part of the project ran from 1999 to 2001. The Honeynet Project identified, tracked, and discussed different types of attacks and probes with Gen I honeynets (discussed later in this chapter). Its main objective was to identify the most common threats against default installations of operating systems and applications.
- *Phase II*: This phase ran from 2002 to 2003. Its main objective was to develop a better version of a honeynet that was easier to deploy, harder to detect, and more efficient in collecting data. It was directed toward more sophisticated attackers.
- *Phase III*: This phase was initiated in 2004. Its main objective was to make a bootable CD-ROM that boots into a honeynet gateway, or a **honeywall**. After booting, it makes a gateway outside the system or network through which all information is required to pass. The bootable devices are easier to apply and have the option of logging on to a central system.
- *Phase IV*: This phase was also initiated in 2004, and its goal was to make a centralized system that gathers and correlates data from distributed honeynets.

## Types of Honeynets

### Distributed Honeynet

Distributed honeynets use open-source software to implement IDS over a network. Distributed honeynets help develop, deploy, and analyze the data from a network of multiple honeynets controlled by a single organization, as shown in Figure 4-5.

### Gen I Honeynet

The Gen I honeynet was first developed in 1999 to improve the then-current honeypot technologies. It has the ability to gather more information than a standard honeypot and can identify unknown attacks. It not only provides data capture methods but can also control and maintain attackers. The architecture of the Gen I honeynet is shown in Figure 4-6.

The main data-control device that controls the Gen I architecture is a conventional firewall with honeynet policies. Honeynet policies are combined with two mechanisms to provide an effective data-control architecture: connection blocking and connection limiting.

Connection blocking is used to block excessive connections between the honeynet and outside systems. This mechanism creates a firewall rule base that allows only limited connections and blocks remaining connections that exceed the limit. The rule base required for a Gen I honeynet is implemented by easily managed checkpoint firewalls.

Connection limiting is mainly used to limit the bandwidth for inbound and outbound connections, which can slow down the operations of attackers.

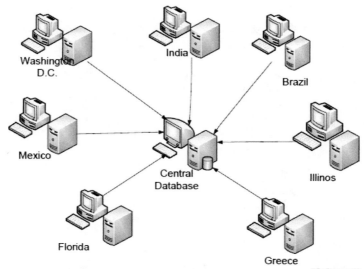

**Figure 4-5**   A distributed honeynet is a network of honeynets controlled by a central database.

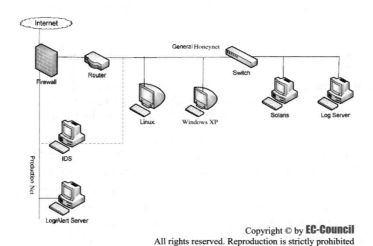

**Figure 4-6**   The Gen I honeynet is the first-generation honeynet.

The three important layers of the Gen I honeynet are the firewall, IDS, and syslog/Trojaned shell.

- A firewall controls and captures the data. This includes inbound and outbound connections, ports, IP addresses of both source and destination, and the date and time of attack.
- The IDS layer captures packet payloads from honeynet researchers.
- Syslog and Trojaned shell is the third layer that captures data from honeypots. By modifying honeypots, it will be easy to capture the attacker's keystrokes, which are processed here.

Technologies used in the Gen I honeynet architecture include syslog, remote syslog servers, and Trojaned bash shells, which are predominant in UNIX servers.

## Gen II and Gen III Honeynets

The Gen II honeynet was developed in 2001, and the Gen III honeynet was introduced at the end of 2004. The architecture of these two honeynets is quite similar, and Gen III has improved in deployment and management.

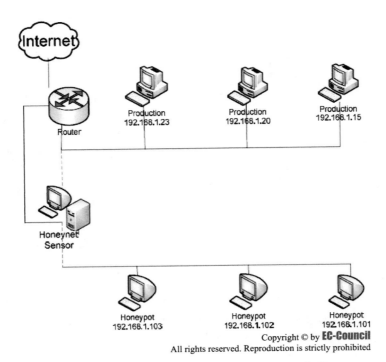

**Figure 4-7**   Gen II and Gen III honeynets are very similar.

To overcome the limitations of Gen I, an IDS gateway was developed for Gen II. The architecture of Gen II is shown in Figure 4-7.

Both of these honeynets combine the features of a firewall and an IDS into a single device called an IDS gateway or a honeywall. The honeynet uses this single device to control the data and also uses sensors to deploy and manage the data. Data control in Gen II and Gen III uses the following three modes:

- Connection-rate limiting mode is similar to Gen I. A firewall is used to control or limit the number of outgoing connections from each honeypot. The difference from Gen I is that in this mechanism, a threshold will be used that can monitor up to 50 connections every three hours.

- Packet-drop mode is the primary mode for both Gen II and Gen III. This mode provides an intelligent data mechanism, dropping packets that match the signature database. This mechanism can be implemented by using Snort inline, which is a popular type of Snort IDS. Through this, Snort inline mechanisms with only outgoing packets will be checked and dropped.

- Packet-replace mode works much like packet-drop mode, but instead of dropping the whole packet, it uses Snort inline to modify the parts of the packets that are less harmful. This mode is quite complicated and requires more knowledge in finding actual attacks and in writing Snort inline rules.

The IDS gateway acts as a network sniffer and logger to capture network traffic. Gen II and Gen III also contain three different layers of data capture, similar to the Gen I architecture:

- The firewall layer is similar to the one in the Gen I architecture.

- The IDS layer checks every packet with a signature database and processes all inbound and outbound packets for future use.

- Honeypot data capture is the last layer. It captures system log and keystroke activities. System logs are monitored to trace the processes that are running in the honeynet during the attack.

## Virtual Honeynet

A virtual honeynet takes various honeynet technologies and implements them in a single computer. This could be either a self-contained virtual honeynet or a hybrid virtual honeynet.

*Self-Contained Virtual Honeynet* This honeynet contains a honeypot, a firewall gateway, and data control for data capture, all in a single computer.

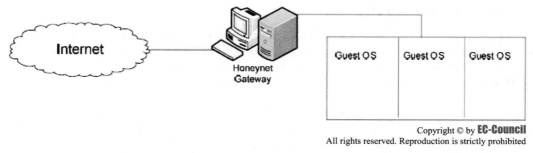

**Figure 4-8**  A hybrid virtual honeynet combines a classic honeynet with virtual software.

A self contained virtual honeynet has the following advantages:

- This honeynet is portable in nature. It can be placed on a laptop and taken anywhere.
- It has a plug-and-patch feature that allows it to be taken from one box and plugged into any network.
- It has a low cost, occupies less space for data storage, and consumes less power.

However, it also has the following disadvantages:

- If hardware fails, then the entire system will fail to operate.
- It requires a high-quality computer with a good deal of memory and a fast processor.
- Security is not provided to other parts of the system. This provides an opportunity for attackers to strike those other parts.
- Software usage is limited.

*Hybrid Virtual Honeynet*  A hybrid virtual honeynet is a combination of a classic honeynet and virtual software, and is shown in Figure 4-8. Data-control services, like IDS sensors, and logging and data-capture services, such as firewalls, are placed separately in an isolated system.

Advantages of a hybrid virtual honeynet include:

- Highly secured
- Highly flexible

Disadvantages of a hybrid virtual honeynet include:

- Difficult to relocate
- Expensive in terms of both time and space

## U.S. Legal Issues Related to Honeynets

### The Fourth Amendment

If a honeynet is operated under the direction of the government, the Fourth Amendment to the United States Constitution may apply. The Fourth Amendment limits the power of government agents to search for evidence without having first secured a search warrant. Evidence seized in violation of the Fourth Amendment may not be admissible at a criminal trial. In addition, the person who violated the Fourth Amendment rights of another may be subject to a lawsuit for monetary damages.

However, the Fourth Amendment applies only to a person entitled to a "reasonable expectation of privacy." Those who hack into networks are not likely to have a "reasonable" expectation of privacy in their use of the victim network. In addition, the Fourth Amendment restricts searches only by the government; a private firm may deploy a honeynet and monitor users without worrying about the Fourth Amendment, unless said firm is working directly with the government. Similar provisions in state constitutions are at least as rigorous as the federal Constitution.

### The Federal Wiretap Act

The Federal Wiretap Act generally forbids the interception of the content of communications (including electronic communications) unless one of the exceptions listed in the statute applies. Sniffing traffic on a network is considered an interception of electronic communications and falls within the scope of this act. Violation of the Wiretap Act can lead to a civil suit and may constitute a federal felony punishable by a fine and up to five years in prison.

If the honeynet is not configured to capture the content of communications of users, the Wiretap Act does not apply. For example, a low-interaction honeynet could be configured to only log the IP addresses and port calls of incoming connection attempts, but not the content of the communications.

### The Pen Register/Trap and Trace Statute

The Pen Register/Trap and Trace statute (Pen/Trap statute) governs the real-time collection of noncontent traffic information associated with communications, such as the phone numbers dialed by a particular telephone or the destination or source IP address of a computer network user. The statute refers to this data as "dialing, routing, addressing, or signaling information." Like the Wiretap Act's prohibition on the interception of the contents of communications, the Pen/Trap statute prohibits the real-time monitoring of traffic data. A pen register is a device or process that records outgoing connection information (for example, the telephone number dialed from a monitored telephone), while a trap-and-trace device captures incoming connection information (for example, the phone number of a call to the monitored telephone).

The Pen/Trap statute generally forbids the acquisition of communication information, unless one of the listed exceptions applies. These exceptions include network routing information, such as the source and destination IP address, the port number that handled that communication, and e-mail addresses of the attackers. If the device or process is intended to capture the content of communications, such as the subject line or body of an e-mail or the content of a downloaded file, then its use is governed by the Wiretap Act, not by the Pen/Trap statute.

The statute has never been tested in court as applied to honeynets. Providers are permitted to use Pen/Trap devices as follows:

- Relating to the operation, maintenance, and testing of a wire or electronic communication service or to the protection of the rights or property of such provider, or to the protection of users of that service from abuse of service or unlawful use of service

- To record the fact that a wire or electronic communication was initiated or completed in order to protect such provider, another provider furnishing service toward the completion of the wire communication, or a user of that service from fraudulent, unlawful, or abusive use of service

- When the consent of the user has been obtained

# Chapter Summary

- A bastion host acts as a gateway between an internal private network and the outside public network. It is placed on the unrestricted side of the demilitarized zone (DMZ), so it is completely exposed to an attack.
- There are several types of bastion hosts, including the following: nonrouting dual-homed hosts, victim machines, internal bastion hosts, external services hosts, and one-box firewalls.
- Honeypots are servers placed on a network to entice attackers to target the honeypot instead of real production systems.
- Honeypots are classified into two types: production honeypots and research honeypots.
- Low-interaction honeypots detect unauthorized access and system scans.
- Medium-interaction honeypots allow the attacker to advance, gathering details of the attack for analysis and reporting.
- Honeynets are examples of high-interaction honeypots. They are very complex and are difficult to build, deploy, and configure.
- The rules, regulations, and laws of using honeypots vary in different countries. Legal concerns include the need for data collection, the way is the data are used, and the types of data collected.

# Review Questions

1. What is a bastion host?

_____

_____

_____

_____

2. What are the general requirements to set up a bastion host?

_____

_____

_____

_____

3. What are the steps that should be followed to build a bastion host?

_____

_____

_____

_____

4. How is a bastion host configured?

_____

_____

_____

_____

5. What is a honeypot?

_____

_____

_____

_____

6. What is the difference between a production honeypot and a research honeypot?

_____

_____

_____

_____

7. What is a low-interaction honeypot?

_____

_____

_____

_____

8. What is a high-interaction honeypot?

_____

_____

_____

_____

9. What is a port-monitoring honeypot?

_____

_____

_____

_____

10. What is a jailed honeypot?

_____

_____

_____

_____

11. What is ManTrap?

_____

_____

_____

_____

12. What is a honeynet?

_____

_____

_____

_____

13. What are the different types of honeynets?

_____

_____

_____

_____

# Hands-On Projects

1. Use the MwWatcher honeypot to watch the file system for suspicious activity caused by malware infections in real time.

   ■ Navigate to Chapter 4 of the Student Resource Center.

   ■ Install and launch the MwWatcher program.

   ■ Start MwWatcher and review the notifications.

2. Perform the following steps:

   ■ Navigate to Chapter 4 of the Student Resource Center.

   ■ Open Understanding Network Threats through Honeypot Deployment.pdf and read the content.

3. Perform the following steps:

   ■ Navigate to Chapter 4 of the Student Resource Center.

   ■ Open Definitions and Value of Honeypots.pdf and read the content.

4. Perform the following steps:

   ■ Navigate to Chapter 4 of the Student Resource Center.

   ■ Open Honeypots Revealed.pdf and read the content.

5. Perform the following steps:

   ■ Navigate to Chapter 4 of the Student Resource Center.

   ■ Open Cyberlaw Honeypot Edition.pdf and read the content.

# Chapter 5

# Wireless Network Security

## Objectives

**After completing this chapter, you should be able to:**

- Understand the components of a wireless network
- Understand wireless technologies
- Detect wireless networks
- Understand wireless threats and attacks
- Understand wireless standards
- Secure wireless communications
- Develop a wireless security policy
- Manage certificates through PKI
- Develop a wireless network security checklist

## Key Terms

**roaming** the action of moving between wireless coverage areas with no interruption in service

## Introduction to Wireless Network Security

Wireless networking is quickly replacing traditional wired networking as the norm, both in the home and in the workplace. While it has several advantages, such as greatly increased mobility, there are also added security risks associated with transmitting data wirelessly. Because it is sent over the air, it is much easier for a third party to intercept the data in transit, so extra security precautions must be taken. This chapter teaches you about wireless networks and what it takes to make them secure.

## Wired Networks Versus Wireless Networks

Table 5-1 shows the differences between wired networks and wireless networks.

| Wired Networks | Wireless Networks |
|---|---|
| High bandwidth | Low bandwidth |
| Low bandwidth variation | High bandwidth variation |
| Low error rates ($10^{-6}$) | High error rates ($10^{-3}$) |
| More secure | Less secure |
| Less equipment dependent | More equipment dependent |
| Symmetric connectivity | Possible asymmetric connectivity |
| Primarily used by high-power machines | Primarily used by low-power machines |
| Low delay | Higher delay |
| Connected operation | Disconnected operation |

**Table 5-1**    **These are the main differences between wired networks and wireless networks**

Wireless networks have the following advantages over wired networks:

- High mobility
- Easily connected
- The initial cost of setting up a WLAN is significantly lower than manually cabling an entire enterprise
- Data can be transmitted in different ways through cellular networks, Mobitex, DataTAC, Cellular Digital Packet Data (CDPD), etc.
- Sharing of data is easy between wireless devices

However, they also have the following disadvantages:

- No physical security
- Packets are sent through air, so an attacker can use wireless sniffing tools
- Most wireless standards use a wide spectrum, so it is very simple to identify the signal, making it more susceptible to hackers

# Wireless Network Types

## Types Based on Connection

### *Peer-to-Peer Networks*

In this network, every computer communicates directly with all other computers on the network without the use of a common access point. The computers can share files and printers, but they may not be able to access wired LAN sources unless one of the computers uses special software to act as a bridge to the wired LAN. Figure 5-1 shows a peer-to-peer network.

### *Extension to a Wired Network*

A wired network can be extended by placing access points between the wired network and wireless devices. This network can also include an access point, or base station, acting as a hub. It can connect the wireless LAN to a wired LAN, which allows wireless devices to access LAN resources, such as file servers or existing Internet connectivity.

There are both software and hardware access points available. Software access points run on a computer with a wireless network interface card. Hardware access points (HAPs) provide comprehensive support of most wireless features.

### *Multiple Access Points*

If an area is too large to be covered by a single access point, multiple access points can be used. While using multiple access points, each access point's wireless area must cover its neighbors. This allows users to move around a seamless area using a feature called *roaming*, which involves moving between wireless coverage areas with no interruption in service. Some manufacturers develop extension points, which act as wireless relays, extending

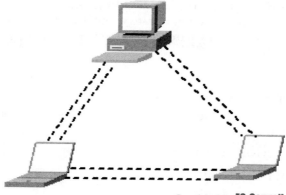

**Figure 5-1** In a peer-to-peer network, computers directly communicate with one another without an access point.

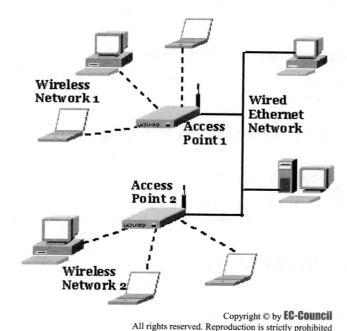

**Figure 5-2** Wireless networks can use multiple access points to cover larger areas.

the range of a single access point. Multiple extension points can be strung together to give wireless access to far-away locations from a central access point. Figure 5-2 shows a network with multiple wireless access points.

### LAN-to-LAN Wireless Network

Hardware access points have the ability to directly connect with other hardware access points. Interconnecting LANs using wireless connections can be a large and complex task.

## Types Based on Area Covered

### WLAN (Wireless Local Area Network)

A wireless local area network (WLAN) connects wireless users to form a local area network using high-frequency radio waves. The area may range from a single room to an entire campus. This is also known as a local area wireless network (LAWN).

A WLAN can exist in peer-to-peer mode or infrastructure mode. In peer-to-peer mode, wireless devices within range of each other directly communicate without using central access points. In infrastructure mode, there is a central access point, usually wired to the Internet and perhaps a wired LAN.

Advantages of a WLAN include:

- Flexible
- Very easy to set up and use
- Can be robust; if one base station is down, users may be able to physically move their PCs to be in range of another base station
- Better chance of surviving a disaster

Disadvantages of a WLAN include:

- Lower speed than wired networks
- Wired networks are easier to secure

### WWAN (Wireless Wide Area Network)

This covers an area larger than a WLAN using cellular network technology such as CDMA, GSM, GPRS, and CDPD. This technology may cover a particular region, nation, or even the entire globe. Users use a cellular radio (GSM/CDMA) to send or receive data. This includes cell phones, satellite links, global positioning systems (GPS), and more.

### WPAN (Wireless Personal Area Network)

A WPAN interconnects the devices positioned around an individual. These networks have a short range, usually about 10 meters. The current most popular standard for WPAN is Bluetooth. A WPAN can lock out other devices and prevent unusual interference.

### WMAN (Wireless Metropolitan Area Network)

A WMAN covers a very large area, such as an entire city or suburb. It accesses broadband area networks by using exterior antennas. Subscriber stations communicate with the base station, which is connected to a central network or hub. WMAN uses a wireless infrastructure or optical fiber connections to link WLANs. Distributed queue dual bus (DQDB), specified by IEEE 802.6, is the WMAN standard for data communications. Using DQDB, a network can be established over 30 miles long with a speed of 34 to 154 Mbps.

# Components of a Wireless Network

## Antenna

An antenna is designed to transmit and receive electromagnetic waves, usually radio waves. It is a collection of metal rods and wires that capture radio waves and translate them into electrical current. The size and shape of antennas are designed according to the frequency of the signal the antennas are designed to receive.

A high-gain antenna is highly focused, while a low-gain antenna receives or transmits over a large angle. A transducer translates radio-frequency fields into AC current and vice versa. Antennas can be either omnidirectional or directional.

### Directional Versus Omnidirectional

Directional antennas radiate radio waves in a more constrained area. They are not as versatile as omnidirectional antennas, but are useful for fixed locations. These antennas are used where the distance between the transmitter and receiver is no more than a few hundred meters. The wavelength used in these antennas is very small, so they can be used to transfer large amounts of information. The following are some characteristics of directional antennas:

- Directional antennas are designed for the purpose of concentrating the radio signals in a particular direction.
- The directivity of an antenna determines how the RF energy is focused.
- The amount of RF energy remains constant but spreads over a small area, so the signal strength is higher. The antenna gain is measured in decibels or in dipole (dBd).

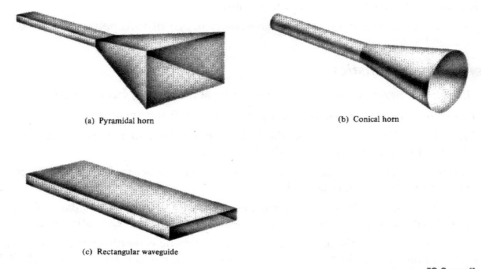

(a) Pyramidal horn                    (b) Conical horn

(c) Rectangular waveguide

**Figure 5-3**   Other examples of aperture antennas include parabolic reflector, horn, lenses, and circular.

Omnidirectional antennas radiate electromagnetic energy uniformly in all directions. They usually radiate strong waves in two dimensions, but not as strongly in the third. These antennas are effective for covering areas where the locations of other wireless stations will vary with time. For example, radio stations use omnidirectional antennas, because the receivers may not be stationary.

## Aperture Versus Leaky Wave

Aperture antennas have a physical opening through which electromagnetic waves propagate. These antennas are developed from waveguide technology. The particular pattern has a short main beam that denotes high gain. These antennas are suitable for a frequency range between 1 and 20 GHz.

For a fixed aperture size, the main beam pattern becomes short as the frequency increases. These types of antennas are used in aircraft and spacecraft applications. Figure 5-3 shows some examples of aperture antennas.

Leaky wave antennas are obtained from millimeter waves (mm-wave) like dielectric guides, microstrip lines, coplanar lines, and slot lines. These antennas are used for applications with frequencies of more than 30 GHz, including infrared. Periodic breaks are established at the end of guides, resulting in large radiation leakage.

## Reflector Antennas

Reflector antennas are used to concentrate electromagnetic energy that is radiated or received at a focal point. These reflectors are generally parabolic. A parabolic cylinder mirror transmits the rays from a main line source into a group of parallel rays. These are often used in radio telescopes and satellite communication.

Large reflectors have the following characteristics:

- High gain and directivity
- Difficult to manufacture
- Mechanically weak
- Heavy

Plain reflectors will maintain a radio link without a line of sight.

## Antenna Parts

All antennas have the following parts:

- *Transmission line*: Antennas transmit or receive radio waves from one point to another. This power transmission takes place in free space through natural media like air, water, and earth.

- *Radiator*: This part radiates the energy through the medium.
- *Resonator*: The use of a resonator is necessary in broadband applications. Resonances that occur must be attenuated.

### Antenna Characteristics

- *Operating frequency band*: Antennas operate at a frequency band of between 960 MHz and 1215 MHz.
- *Transmit power*: Antennas transmit power at a 1200-watt peak and a 140-watt average.
- *Typical gain*: Gain is the ratio of the power input to the antenna versus the power output from the antenna. The gain is measured in decibels (dBi).
- *Radiation pattern*: The radiation pattern of an antenna is in a 3-D plot. This pattern generally takes two forms: elevation and azimuth.
- *Directivity*: Directivity gain is the calculation of radiated power in a particular direction. It is generally the ratio of radiation intensity in a given direction to the average radiation intensity.
- *Polarization*: This is the orientation of electromagnetic waves from the source. There are a number of polarizations such as linear, vertical, horizontal, circular, left-hand circular (LHCP), and right-hand circular (RHCP).

## Access Points

Access points are either hardware devices or software used to connect wireless users to a wired network. An access point, also called an AP or a base station, acts as a bridge or hub between the wired LAN and the wireless network. APs are necessary for providing strong wireless security, as well as increasing the physical range of the network. The range can be further increased with the help of repeaters, which amplify the network's radio signals.

### Operating Modes of Access Points

- In access-point mode, an AP acts as a hub or a station to which wireless clients can connect. An AP should be hardwired to a switch or other node.
- In repeater mode, APs work to increase the range of the wireless network. Repeaters receive signals from an AP, amplify that network's radio signals, and transmit them to wireless clients.
- Bridge mode is used for connecting two separate LAN networks for communication. As always, APs must be wired to a switch or other network device.
- A multipoint bridge is formed when more than two access points are connected to each other to form a wireless link.
- In wireless-client mode, an AP provides a wireless connection between two LANs.

## PC Cards

A PC card is a credit card–sized peripheral that adds memory, mass storage, and I/O capabilities to a computer. A PC card interface uses ISA-style or PCI parallel bus connections, using 68 contact pins and a socket connector. Throughput of the PC card interface is as follows:

- CardBus (32-bit burst mode)
  - Byte mode: 33 Mbps
  - Word mode: 66 Mbps
  - DWord mode: 132 Mbps
- 16-bit memory transfer (100-ns minimum cycle)
  - Byte mode: 10 Mbps
  - Word mode: 20 Mbps
- 16-bit I/O transfer (255-ns minimum cycle)
  - Byte mode: 3.92 Mbps
  - Word mode: 7.84 Mbps

The PC card standard provides three types of PC cards (Types I, II, and III), which have the same length and width and use the same 68-pin connector, but have different thicknesses. A thin card can be used in a thick slot, but a thick card cannot be used in a thin slot.

The PC card standard defines the operation of PC cards at two different voltages: 3.3 V and 5.0 V. To prevent 3.3 V cards from being inserted into 5.0 V slots, a key is located on the edge of the PC card connector that operates only at 5.0 V.

### Applications of PC Cards

- Type I PC cards are used for memory devices such as RAM, flash, OTP (one-time password), and SRAM cards.

- Type II PC cards are used for I/O devices like data/fax modems, LANs, and mass-storage devices.

- Type III PC cards are used for devices whose components are thicker, such as rotating mass-storage devices.

- Extended cards are used for components that must remain outside the system for appropriate operation, like antennas for wireless applications.

## Wireless Cards

Wireless network cards locate and communicate with access points. Wireless network cards should be Wi-Fi certified by the Wireless Ethernet Compatibility Alliance (WECA). Because wireless standards change, it is important to keep the card's firmware updated. A wireless network interface card (WNIC), unlike other network cards, works only with an 802.11 network. A WNIC works in the physical and data-link layers of the OSI model. A WNIC is a fundamental component for wireless desktop computers. The WNIC in a desktop PC is generally located in the PCI slot.

A WNIC can function in infrastructure mode or ad hoc mode. In infrastructure mode, the WNIC connects to an access point. It then sends data to other wireless nodes through the access point, which acts as a central hub. While linking to an access point using infrastructure mode, the WNIC must use the same service set identifier (SSID) as the access point. If the access point is configured for WEP, then the same WEP key or other authentication field must be provided.

In ad hoc mode, the WNIC does not need an access point, as it can directly interface with all other wireless computers. When configuring the node in ad hoc mode, all other nodes must use the same channel and SSID.

## Wireless Modem

A wireless modem uses cellular, satellite, or Wi-Fi protocols to connect to a WLAN. Wireless modems can connect to a computer through PCMCIA, USB, serial, or PCI ports. They support various protocols and frequency bands over a number of channels.

## Wireless Router

A wireless router connects the network together and operates at the network layer of the OSI model. It is a regular IP router with 802.11 interfaces and an antenna. Connected users can share files, pictures, peripherals, printers, and more with everyone on the network. They are not as secure as wired routers.

## Wireless USB

Wireless USB connects peripherals and consumer electronic devices to a host PC. It is based on ultrawideband (UWB) technology that supports a 480-Mbps data rate over a distance of two meters. If the speed is lowered to 110 Mbps, then UWB is able to go about 10 meters. This technology is good for both home and office environments.

Wireless USB uses a hub-and-spoke topology. The host initiates all data traffic among the devices that are connected to it, assigning time slots and data bandwidth to each device. These relationships are referred to as clusters. The connections between the wireless USB host and wireless USB devices are point-to-point and direct. A wireless USB host connects a maximum of 127 wireless USB devices.

Wireless USB technology has the following attributes:

- Simple and low-cost implementation

- Point-to-point connection topology that supports up to 127 devices, following the same host-to-device architecture used for wired USB

- Consists of high spatial capacity in small areas, which allows access to multiple devices concurrently at high bandwidth
- Uses a dual-role model where each device has limited host capabilities, allowing mobile devices to access services with a central host
- Easy to connect wireless USB devices and hosts
- Mutual authentication in device and host connections
- Includes world-class security as a standard
- Includes an asymmetric host-centric model that maintains the USB model of cheap or simple devices and confines the complexity to the host

## Wireless Print Server

A wireless print server allows one or more printers to be shared across a Wi-Fi network. A wireless print server can connect to a wireless router over Wi-Fi itself or can be attached using an Ethernet cable.

To complete the configuration of the device, print servers usually contain setup software on a CD-ROM to be installed on a computer. The print server needs client software to be installed on every computer. Often, this software is installed automatically, without user intervention, when the printer is added to the client computer.

Advantages of a wireless print server include:

- Allows users to place printers anywhere within the range of a wireless network
- Does not require a computer to be on in order to print
- Does not require a computer to manage all print jobs
- Administrators can change computer names and settings without reconfiguring the network printing settings

## Wireless Range Extender

A wireless range extender increases the distance over which a WLAN signal can be broadcast. Different forms of wireless range extenders are available in the form of range expanders or signal boosters. These devices work as communication or network repeaters, selecting and reflecting Wi-Fi signals from a network's base router or access point.

## Wireless Internet Video Cameras

A wireless Internet video camera allows video and audio data to be recorded and transmitted through a Wi-Fi computer network. It contains a built-in Web server, so computers can easily connect to it by using either a standard Web browser or a special client user interface. These cameras are connected through wireless routers either wirelessly or using Ethernet cables.

Features of wireless Internet video cameras include:

- Some contain motion sensors, which have the ability to send e-mail alerts when new activity is detected and captured
- Can time-stamp images
- Contain built-in microphones and jacks for external microphones and audio support
- Support Wi-Fi security such as WEP or WAP

## GSM Network Devices

Global System for Mobile Communication (GSM) is a cellular network. GSM is different from previous cellular networks because both signaling and speech are transmitted in digital form. As in other cellular networks, GSM supports roaming, allowing the user to use the same phone all over the world. Most GSM networks operate in the 900-MHz or 1800-MHz bands. GSM uses a variant of linear predictive coding (LPC), which reduces the bit rate. It also uses the Gaussian minimum shift keying (GMSK) type of modulation.

A GSM network system consists of the following devices:

- Mobile station
- Base station subsystem
    - Base station controller
    - Base transceiver station
- Network subsystem
    - Mobile switching center
    - Home location register
    - Visitor location register
    - Authentication center
    - Equipment identity register

## Mobile Station (MS)

A mobile station (MS) includes mobile equipment (ME) and the subscriber identity module (SIM). The mobile stations communicate with the base transceiver station (BTS) in the base station system (BSS) through the Um interface (air interface). The ME is a physical device like telephones and PCs. Each ME is individually identified with the International Mobile Equipment Identity (IMEI).

The MS contains the SIM. The SIM is a small card that contains the telephone number of the subscriber, encoded network identification details, a PIN, and many other pieces of user information such as the phonebook. It contains all the information that is necessary to activate the phone. The SIM also contains the International Mobile Subscriber Identity (IMSI).

*MExE (Mobile Station Application Execution Environment)* MExE allows for the secure download of applications for mobile computing and e-commerce purposes. It includes a complete application environment for mobile devices containing Java Virtual Machine (JVM). MExE describes various technology requirements known as classmarks:

- Classmark 1 is based on Wireless Application Protocol (WAP). It provides simple and cheap data access over a slow-or high-latency link.
- Classmark 2 is based on a personal Java environment and Java phones. It uses standard Internet technology. It provides strong applications and flexible MMIs (man-machine interfaces).
- Classmark 3 is based on the CLDC and MIDP applications of J2ME.

## Base Station Subsystem (BSS)

A base station subsystem (BSS) consists of two main components: the base station controller (BSC) and the base transceiver station (BTS). The BTS and BSC communicate through the Abis interface. The BTS contains the radio transceiver that describes the cell and handles the radio link protocols. Wide areas require multiple BTSs, so it is necessary that they be rugged, reliable, portable, and low cost.

*Base Station Controller (BSC)* The base station controller is the part of the base station subsystem that communicates with the base transceiver station through the Abis interface. The BSC controls one or more cell sites' radio signals, thus reducing the load on the switch. The BSC connects the mobile station and mobile service switching center (MSC).

The BSC is used for:

- Handling the radio sources for one or several BTSs
- Managing the radio-channel setup and frequency hopping
- Managing the handover technique

*Base Transceiver Station (BTS)* The BTS contains an antenna and transceiver that handle the radio interface with a mobile phone communication system. It is the first thing that detects a mobile signal. It communicates with mobile phones and PCS phones.

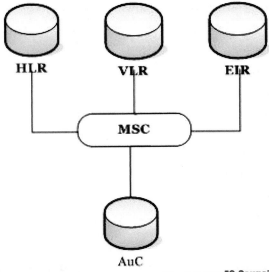

**Figure 5-4** A network subsystem links the cellular network and the public telephone network.

The BTS connects to a BSC over a T1/E1 line, which encrypts and decrypts the communication. The signal strength of the BTS defines how much coverage is available.

A BTS contains many transceivers that allow for several different frequencies and sectors of the cell. Distinctive BTS sites contain between 1 and 12 transceivers in one, two, or three sectors, though these numbers vary widely. It is kept under control by the parent BSC over Base Station Control Function (BCF), making the functions of each BTS differ from vendor to vendor.

BTSs are equipped with radios that modulate the layers of the air interface. To increase the performance of the BTS, frequency hopping is used, which increases the voice traffic between transceivers in a sector.

### Network Subsystem

The network subsystem (NS) acts as a link between a cellular network and a public switched telephone network (PSTN) or public switched data network (PSDN). The mobile switching center (MSC) is the main element of the NS. Services like registration, authentication, location updating, and handover are provided with different parts of the NS. Figure 5-4 shows a network subsystem.

*Mobile Switching Center* The mobile switching center (MSC) is the part of the GSM system that performs switching functions and handles communication between the public telephone system and mobile phones. MSCs are defined by various names according to their functions:

- A gateway MSC (GMSC) detects the current MSC called by a subscriber. Mobile-to-mobile and mobile-to-PSDN calls are routed through a GMSC.
- A visited MSC is the MSC where a user is currently located.
- An anchor MSC is where the handover is given.
- A target MSC is where the handover is received.

An MSC provides the following functionality:

- An MSC with an HLR (home location register) and a VLR (visitor location register) provides the call routing and roaming abilities of GSM.
- It also provides the functions necessary for managing mobile subscriber registration, authentication, and location updating.
- It handles the mobility management operations.

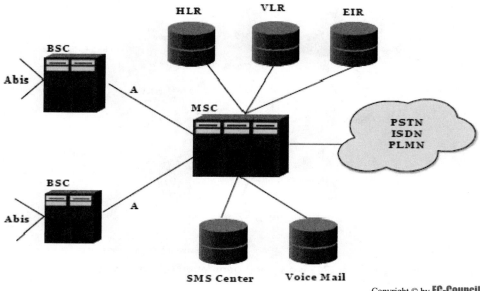

**Figure 5-5** A mobile switching center communicates between the cellular network and the PSTN.

A mobile switching center contains the following databases:

- The home location register (HLR) database contains information about the subscriber that is recorded in the respective GSM network, along with the current location of the mobile device. This location generally takes the form of a signaling address. There is one HLR for each GSM network.

- The visitor location register (VLR) database contains only selected information about the subscriber currently in the physical range of the HLR, which is important for call control and provision of subscribed services.

- The authentication center database contains a copy of the secret key present in each subscriber's SIM card; this key is used for authentication and encryption.

- The equipment identity register (EIR) database contains a set of all valid mobile equipment, in which every mobile station is found with the help of its international mobile equipment identity (IMEI).

Figure 5-5 shows a mobile switching center.

# Understanding Wireless Technologies

Wireless technology is used primarily for mobile equipment, such as cellular telephones, personal digital assistants (PDAs), and wireless networking. It also includes GPS units, garage door openers, wireless computer mice and keyboards, satellite television, and cordless telephones.

## Personal Communications Services (PCS)

Personal Communications Services (PCS) are wireless communication services used for cellular phones within the 1900-MHz band. It is a second-generation digital voice, messaging, and data cell phone system, sometimes referred to as digital cellular. For mobile users, PCS requires a number of antennas to cover an area. When a user moves around, the nearest antenna picks up the user's phone signal and forwards it to a base station connected to the wired network.

Figure 5-6 shows a PCS network.

### Dual-Band and Dual-Mode Operation in PCS

Dual-band PCS phones operate at both 800 MHz and 1900 MHz to allow users to receive full PCS features and services while roaming. The dual-mode ability of PCS provides service continuity and interoperability between analog and digital networks.

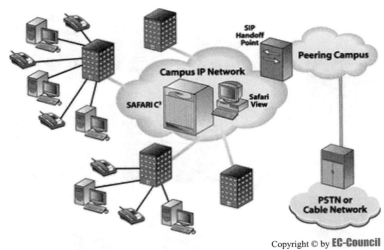

**Figure 5-6** PCS is a second-generation cellular network.

| Feature | Capabilities |
|---|---|
| Sleep mode | Extends phone standby time and improves battery life |
| Simple message service (SMS) | Sends alphanumeric messages to and from cellular and PCS phones |
| Voice and data privacy | Increases resistance to eavesdropping |
| Improved voice quality | Less background noise and fewer dropped calls |
| Intelligent rescan | Allows tighter control of system selection |
| Hierarchical environment | Provides support for macrocell-macrocell operation |
| Seamless roaming | Provides roaming between frequencies using dual-band phones and provides support for international roaming |
| Private and residential system IDs | Provides more simplified and controlled wireless office service (WOS) and personal base station (PBS) features |
| Authentication | Increases phone security and resistance to cloning |
| Circuit-switched data support | Provides highly reliable data transmission for wireless e-mail, faxing, and Internet access |
| Message waiting indicator (MWI) | Notifies users that they have voice mail messages |
| Calling number indication (CNI) | Allows callers to be identified before answering |
| Text dispatch service | Live operators take caller messages and send text messages |

**Table 5-2** These are some of the standard features of PCS

### Features and Capabilities of PCS

Table 5-2 shows some of the features of PCS and their associated capabilities.

## Time Division Multiple Access (TDMA)

Time division multiple access (TDMA), shown in Figure 5-7, is a technology in which digital wireless transmission permits multiple users to use a single radio-frequency channel without interference, by assigning unique time slots to each user within the channel. TDMA sees audio signals divided into millisecond-long packets. It distributes a single frequency channel for a short time and turns to another channel. IS-54 (2G) allows three users to share the same 30-KHz channels, while GSM allows eight users to share the same 270-KHz channels.

Advantages of TDMA include:

- Appropriate for digital communication
- Often gets higher capacity

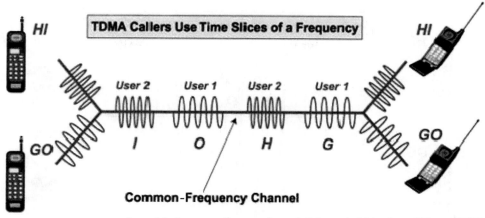

Source: http://www.pangolinsms.com/images/cellular-standards/tdma-large.gif. Accessed 2004.

**Figure 5-7**    TDMA allows multiple users to share a single channel.

- Relaxes need for high-Q filters
- No intermodulation effect
- Throughput remains high for a large number of accesses
- All stations transmit and receive on the same frequency
- Provides the user with extended battery life and talk time
- Provides significant savings in base station equipment, space, and maintenance
- Cost-effective technology for upgrading a current analog system to digital
- Efficient utilization of hierarchical cell structures (HCSs) offering pico, micro, and macro cells

Disadvantages of TDMA include:

- A single time slot is not allotted to a roaming user
- Strict synchronization makes the system more complex
- Guard time needed
- Multipath distortion
- Still vulnerable to jamming and other-cell interference

## Code Division Multiple Access (CDMA)

Code division multiple access (CDMA) is a spread spectrum technology, meaning it does not distribute frequency or time, but instead both parameters can be involved simultaneously. Data transfer is in codes where multiple users use the same time and frequency within the given band/space. It offers better capability, but unwanted signals entering with different codes can spread more noise. It offers efficient voice and data communication, allowing many users to use the airwaves at the same time and use differing technologies. Both 2G and 3G networks use the CDMA air interface. It is the basis for 3G services: the two dominant IMT-2000 standards, CDMA2000 and WCDMA, are based on CDMA.

CDMA is shown in Figure 5-8, and its features include:

- Terminals are connected directly to the system
- Can integrate terminals of dissimilar speeds
- Wide compatibility
- Easy network access
- Efficient line utilization
- Error-free transmission

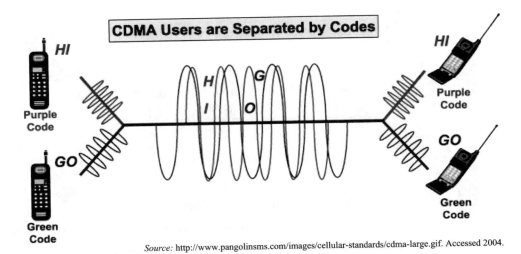

**Figure 5-8**    CDMA separates users by codes.

- Cell frequency reuse
- Soft handoff increases capacity
- Interference is limited
- Narrowband message signal multiplied by wideband spreading signal
- Each user has a unique pseudonoise (PN) code
- Wide bandwidth induces diversity

## Bluetooth

Bluetooth links devices and creates point-to-point or multipoint WPANs (wireless personal area networks). It provides communication between devices at distances of up to 10 meters with access speeds of up to 1 Mbps. It is widely used in mobile computing devices, fixed telecommunications, and consumer equipment using low-cost, miniaturized RF components. It helps share data and voice among various configured devices. Figure 5-9 shows the Bluetooth architecture.

Features of Bluetooth include:

- Operates on the 2.4-GHz ISM band
- Contains a Gaussian frequency-shift-keying modulation scheme
- Transmits data in packets during time slots of fixed duration
- Uses a quick frequency-hopping packet-switched protocol to reduce noise
- Every transceiver has a 48-bit unique address
- Full duplex communication is supported via time division duplex (TDD)
- Able to pass through solid objects
- Omnidirectional
- Three modes of security
- Inexpensive (chips cost about $3)

### Bluetooth Radio and Baseband

The Bluetooth radio is the lowest layer of the Bluetooth specification protocol stack. It defines the requirements of the Bluetooth transceiver device operating in the 2.4-GHz ISM band.

The Bluetooth baseband basically contains a link controller (LC) that carries out baseband protocols and low-layer link routines. Protocols defined within the capability of the baseband specification contain (among others) physical channels and links, error correction and detection, data packet definitions, logical channels, channel control, and hop selection.

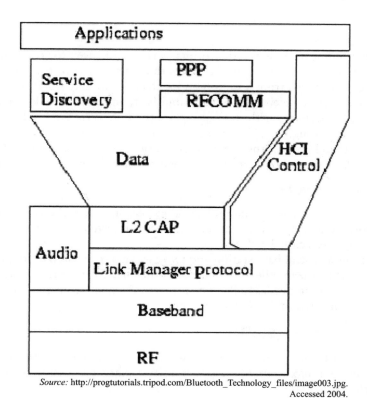

*Source:* http://progtutorials.tripod.com/Bluetooth_Technology_files/image003.jpg.
Accessed 2004.

**Figure 5-9**   This is the architecture of the Bluetooth
standard.

### Bluetooth Software Protocol Stack

This code enables the application software to send and receive information from the Bluetooth module. The major components of the protocol stack are described below.

*Link Manager (LM)* LM manages link setup, link configuration, and link packet control and transfer. It also manages link security at the time of initialization of the connection and throughout the duration of the connection.

*Logical Link Control and Adaptation Protocol (L2CAP)* L2CAP provides services such as protocol multi-plexing, segmentation and reassembly, and quality of service. L2CAP protocol architecture is connection-oriented with connections labeled by a channel identifier. Every channel is assumed to be a full-duplex connection with a quality-of-service (QoS) flow specification when applied to each channel direction.

*Host Control Interface (HCI)* HCI provides a standard interface to the Bluetooth module and link manager services that are independent from the host hardware execution. It also provides precision between the host controller and the Bluetooth hardware.

*Service Discovery Protocol (SDP)* This layer provides high-level services such as LAN access or printer services to users and other applications.

*Audio and Telephony Control* These two protocols are connected, because telephony control in the Bluetooth specification contains call control and audio control. Telephony control provides the interface required to connect and disconnect a call.

*RFCOMM* This protocol emulates RS232 serial ports over Bluetooth to provide compatibility with a large base of applications that currently use the serial port as their main communication bus.

*Human Interface Device (HID)* This includes keyboards, mice, and joysticks, providing plug-and-play support for such devices while used with a PC.

*TCP/IP* TCP/IP is a set of network and transport-layer protocols that is supported by applications and APIs in almost every operating system. Bluetooth uses it to link devices.

## Satellite

A satellite is a communication device that orbits Earth and is used for receiving and transmitting signals. Satellite communication uses electromagnetic waves to transfer data to the satellite from Earth and back again. These signals are transmitted from a station on Earth called an Earth station. The Earth station is dish shaped. Transponders on a satellite receive the signal, amplify it, and send it back to Earth. A satellite has a number of transponders called repeaters. Earth stations receive the signals transmitted by transponders and transmit them to their final receiver through a cable, phone lines, or microwaves.

These satellites travel around the Earth in geostationary orbit, 22,300 miles above the equator. A satellite rotates with the relative speed of Earth in a particular orbit, keeping the antenna in a fixed relative position.

### *Cellular Phone Network*

The cellular phone network is a communication system in which the transmitter and receiver are connected through a microwave to a base transmitter and receiver system. On this network, the world is divided into slightly overlapping areas called cells.

Each cell contains a central base station and two assigned transmission frequencies. The base station uses one set of frequencies, while the mobile phones use the other set. To avoid radio interference, each cell has a different frequency from surrounding cells. Cells at a sufficient distance from each other can have the same frequency. Base stations are connected to a telephone system.

## Service Set Identifier (SSID)

An SSID is the code attached to each packet of wireless data, used to identify which network the packet is using. The code can contain a maximum of 32 alphanumeric characters. All wireless devices that communicate with each other use the same SSID.

# Detecting Wireless Networks

There are many methods used to scan for wireless networks, but the two most often used are wardriving and warchalking.

## Wardriving

Wardriving is used to find available unsecured wireless networks. The attacker takes a device such as a laptop into a car and runs the WNIC in promiscuous mode. He or she also uses software to search for access points. After identifying an open access point, the attacker maps it and explores it. He or she may capture packets to analyze later or run a WEP key cracker on them.

## Warchalking

Warchalking is when, after discovering an open wireless connection, someone will mark on the building or sidewalk a symbol to inform others that there is an available connection. This practice is now also being adopted by those that are sharing networks voluntarily.

## Tool: Kismet

Kismet is a wireless network detector, sniffer, and intrusion detection system. It can be used with any wireless card that supports raw monitoring (rfmon) mode and can sniff 802.11b, 802.11a, and 802.11g traffic. It finds networks by collecting packets and detecting standard-named networks, detecting (and, given time, decloaking) hidden networks, and inferring the occurrence of nonbeaconing networks using data traffic.

## Tool: NetStumbler

NetStumbler is a tool for Windows used to detect WLANs using 802.11b, 802.11a and 802.11g. Its features include the following:

- Verifies that the network is set up the way it was intended
- Finds locations with low coverage in a WLAN
- Detects other networks that are interacting with the target network

- Detects unauthorized rogue access points in a workplace
- Helps to direct antennas for long-haul WLAN links

# Understanding the Various Types of Wireless Threats and Attacks

## Types of Wireless Attacks

Due to the broadcasting feature of wireless networks, they are significantly more vulnerable to attacks than are wired networks.

### Man-In-The-Middle Attack

In a man-in-the-middle attack, the attacker intercepts identification information sent between two parties and uses that information to gain access to the system or to simply gather all data sent.

*Eavesdropping* Eavesdropping is significantly easier in a wireless network because there is no physical medium used for communication. An attacker close to the wireless network can intercept the network's radio waves without too much effort. Data frames sent across the network can be examined in real time or stored for later assessment. In order to prevent hackers from gaining sensitive information, it is necessary to implement several layers of encryption, such as WEP, IPSec, SSH, and SSL. Unfortunately, WEP can be cracked with freely available tools. Accessing e-mail using the POP or IMAP protocols is risky, as these protocols pass the messages over the wireless network without any form of extra encryption. A determined hacker can potentially log giga-bytes worth of WEP-protected traffic in an effort to postprocess the data and break the protection. This makes the wireless network more vulnerable to eavesdropping.

*Manipulation* Manipulation is when an attacker receives the victim's encrypted data, modifies it, and passes on the changed data. The attacker can change e-mails, database transactions, instant messages, or anything else sent over a wireless connection.

### Denial-Of-Service Attacks

Wireless DoS attacks are divided into three types, described in the following three sections.

*Physical DoS Attacks* To conduct a physical DoS attack on a wired network, close proximity with the victim's network is needed. However, in the case of a wireless network, attackers can launch attacks from miles away. Unlike with a wired network, there is no evidence of a wireless physical DoS attack.

The 802.11 PHY (physical layer) specifications define a limited range of frequencies for communication. An attacker can easily make an inexpensive device that saturates the 802.11 frequency bands with noise. In fact, there are several commercial devices available today that can bring down a wireless network with ease. Many 2.4-GHz cordless phones available in the market have the capability to bring down an 802.11b network. These phones can introduce noise that can drop the signal-to-noise ratio to an unusable level. If there is interference in a particular band due to too many signals, networks can fail. Devices will not be able to pick out valid network signals from all the random noise being generated and therefore will be unable to communicate.

An attacker attempting a physical DoS attack can also use large-scale Bluetooth deployments.

*Data-Link DoS Attacks* Since the data-link layer is easily accessible, DoS attacks can be done with relative ease. Attackers do not have to worry about WEP being turned on, as it will not prevent the attack. In addition, with WEP turned off the attacker has complete access to the associations between stations and access points, making it simple to block access to the network. If the victim network is not using WEP authentication, then it is vulnerable to spoofed APs.

If an AP is improperly using diversity antennas, the attacker can deny access to clients associated with the AP. Antenna diversity is a mechanism through whichh a single radio uses more than one antenna to overcome multipath fade. If the diversity antennas do not cover the same region of space, the attacker can deny service to associated stations by taking advantage of the improper setup.

*Network DoS Attacks* Because an 802.11 network is a shared medium, a malicious user can flood the network with traffic, denying access to other devices associated with the affected access point. If the network allows any unauthorized user to be associated with the network, then it is more vulnerable to a network layer DoS attack. For example, an attacker can generate a ping (ICMP) to flood the base station.

## Social Engineering

Social engineering is the most common type of network attack. In this attack, the attacker tries to trick people into revealing information regarding a target system's security. This is the hardest to defend against because computers are not involved at all: each individual must be educated to watch out for it.

## WEP Key Cracking

Because WEP keys are passwords, they are vulnerable to the same cracking techniques as any other password. This includes brute-force attacks, dictionary attacks, hybrid attacks, and birthday attacks.

## Rogue Access Points

Unauthorized access points can allow anyone with an 802.11-equipped device onto the corporate network, which can put attackers very close to mission-critical resources. Attackers can find these points using sniffing tools. An administrator should consider an access point a rogue access point if it looks suspicious, then try to locate it using simple techniques like walking around with a wireless access point sniffing device. Sometimes, a rogue access point may be an active access point that is not connected to the corporate network, in which case there is no security threat.

When a rogue access point is found, it is advisable to shut it off immediately. There are two basic methods for locating unauthorized access points: requesting a beacon and sniffing the air.

*Requesting a Beacon* A wireless device can sense the SSIDs used by nearby wireless access points. When the wireless device detects the SSID, it configures itself to connect to the wireless network. When an 802.11b-compliant network card transmits a packet or requests a beacon, all the access points in the vicinity broadcast their availability via an SSID announcement. The problem with this method is that the access point must be configured to respond to these beacon requests, and many organizations turn off this option. For this reason, this method will not be able to find all access points, but it will find many of them.

*Sniffing the Air* Another method of detecting rogue access points is by using wireless sniffing tools. In order to passively capture packets from the air, the receiver on the wireless card has to be turned on in promiscuous mode. The receiver records the information of the sniffed packet, allowing the hacker to deconstruct the packets to find a way to access the network.

# MAC (Media Access Control) Address

A MAC address is the unique hardware address of a network device. When a computer is connected to the Internet, a routing table associates its assigned IP address to the computer's physical MAC address on the LAN.

In 802.11 networks, the MAC sublayer of the data-link layer (DLC) telecommunication protocol uses the MAC address for communication. There are separate MAC sublayers for every physical device. Most 802.11 access points permit the network administrator to view the MAC addresses of currently connected devices.

Figure 5-10 shows a MAC address as seen when using the Windows ipconfig command.

## MAC Sniffing and AP Spoofing

Most vendors have implemented MAC-level access controls on their 802.11 networks, in which the administrator defines a list of approved client MAC addresses. This feature has two options: open or closed. In a closed MAC filter, only listed addresses are allowed to access the network, so only known safe devices can connect. In an open MAC filter, addresses listed in the filter are prevented from accessing the network. This is not always practical in large networks and will only block specific, known troublemakers.

The MAC address does not provide acceptable security because it is both easily understandable and reproducible. Even if WEP is enabled, an attacker can easily sniff MAC addresses because they appear in clear text format. Moreover, it is possible to change the MAC address on a wireless card, so an attacker can spoof a valid MAC address without much effort. When the attacker tries to login with the spoofed MAC address, the legitimate user with the same MAC address gets disconnected from the wireless network.

# Wi-Fi

Wi-Fi refers to the IEEE 802.11 standard radio technology. It includes many standards within various radio frequencies. For example, 802.11b is a standard for wireless LANs that operate in the 2.4-GHz spectrum with a maximum bandwidth of 11 Mbps.

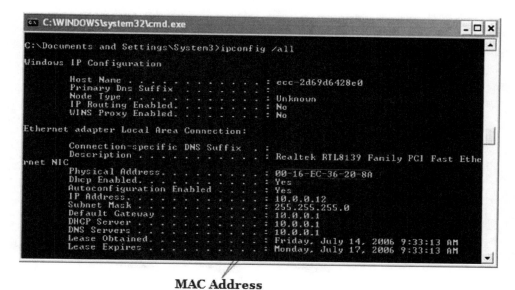

**Figure 5-10**   Every NIC has a unique MAC address.

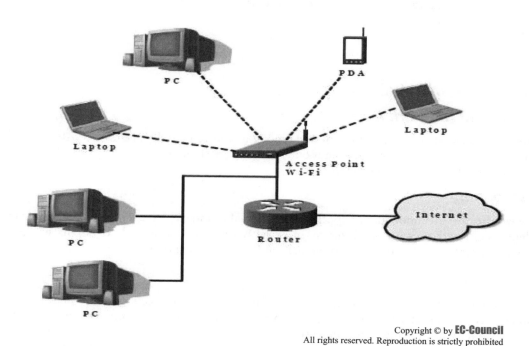

**Figure 5-11**   Wi-Fi is a collection of standards for WLANs.

Wireless technologies must be secured using Wired Equivalent Privacy (WEP), Wi-Fi Protected Access (WPA), Internet Protocol Security (IPSec), or a virtual private network (VPN). They support roaming in between networks and have a fairly low cost of deployment. Figure 5-11 shows a Wi-Fi network.

## Hotspot

A hotspot is an area where public wireless access points are located. Hotspots are used for accessing Internet services via Wi-Fi laptops and other devices that support Wi-Fi. Hotspots are offered in places like hotels, coffee shops, airports, and railway stations. Figure 5-12 shows a hotspot.

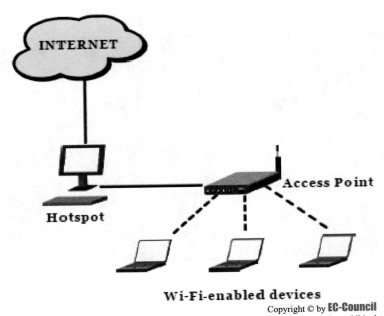

**Figure 5-12**   Hotpots are areas covered by public wireless access points.

## Open Wi-Fi Vulnerabilities

### Unauthorized Network Access

Unauthorized network access is very common among unsecured wireless networks. Almost all home and business Wi-Fi products come ready to use right out of the box, with no security set by default. It is the responsibility of the administrator to secure the network.

### Eavesdropping

Wi-Fi eavesdropping technologies are both readily available and easy to use. These software packages are often completely legitimate network analyzers used by network administrators to debug networks and to discover rogue access points. Every wireless communication that is not encrypted can be captured and viewed.

## Public Wireless Networks

Before creating a public WLAN, an administrator needs to plan to accommodate multiple connections from individual users and groups of users. A WLAN will often have significantly more connections than a wired one. Using a single network for multiple connections eliminates the interference of radio frequencies, while using a single channel for multiple connections can cause APs to overlap and confuse one another.

### Virtual Local Area Networks

VLANs (virtual local area networks) should be supported by APs to secure a network that enables the use of multiple SSIDs. The VLANs can bind SSIDs individually to the VLAN. The APs can direct wireless users to the appropriate network path with the VLANs. Service providers can also access the same wireless network as users. The AP has a network address table that maps the SSID and the VLAN number. The WLAN should give non-802.1x users access to the Internet. These non-802.1x users are directed to the VLAN by giving them the required credentials through the VLAN number.

A wireless AP capable of IEEE 802.1x and RADIUS is necessary to provide security to the WLAN. WLANs can also charge users a fee for their use, billed by the ISP. Users are usually billed based on the amount of data transferred and the amount of time the user is connected to the WLAN.

### Designs for Scalable and Secure WLAN Solutions

The number of wireless users on a WLAN can increase at any time, so the network's bandwidth should be built to handle the huge amount of traffic on WLANs. Use of VLANs and DMZs helps in meeting the network's security needs.

### Security Vulnerabilities with Public-Access Wireless Networks

Extensive use of wireless devices has increased the vulnerabilities in the WLAN architecture. Mobile users connecting through public access points are vulnerable to attacks. These public networks have three main risks involved:

- Anyone can access them due to public availability.
- They provide a link between users on the network and hackers.
- They use high RF transmission power levels to produce a strong signal, which attackers can intercept.

The following should be considered to avoid these risks:

- Steps must be taken to protect against public threats. The physical location should have adequate security.
- Organizations should guard public resources through security protocols like Transport Layer Security (TLS), which is the IETF version of SSL.
- For protecting private resources, IPSec-compliant VPN solutions must be used for secured connections.

### Securing Wireless Public Network Access

Prior to connecting to the corporate LAN, encryption and access control can be disabled so that the messages pass through the network in their original form without being encrypted. This can lead to intruders scanning laptops and mining confidential data. To avoid this, consider these points:

- Laptops that contain critical information should not be connected to a public network.
- Using a VPN provides better protection.
- A firewall must be placed between the system and the network, with settings set to maximum.
- Regularly use and update virus and spyware scanners.

The following checklist should be followed to ensure wireless network security:

- The security issues of all wireless technology used should be carefully considered.
- All staff members should be aware of these issues.
- Risks should be assessed and analyzed.
- Ensure physical protection of the hardware components of the network.
- AP coverage should be measured to see if it covers the entire area.
- AP channels should differ from others in the neighborhood as much as possible to avoid radio frequency interference.
- Default parameters of the wireless devices should be changed, including the SSID.
- If the APs are ever reset, they must be promptly restored to the proper security settings.
- WLAN products must use encryption and privacy settings.
- Wireless and wired networks must be separated with firewalls.
- Antivirus software should be installed on laptops accessing the wireless network.
- Install personal firewalls on roaming mobile devices.
- Encryption features should be always set to strong.
- MAC access control lists should be deployed.
- APs should have strong administrator passwords.
- Randomly generated passwords should be used for better security.

- Test patches before installing them.
- User authentication should be as strong as possible, preferably using technologies such as biometrics, smart cards, and two-factor authentication.
- DHCP and SNMP should be immediately disabled after use.
- Use read-only privileges for shares on the network.
- RADIUS and Kerberos authentication methods should be used.
- Passwords should be periodically changed and kept private.
- Static IP addressing should be used.
- AP configuration should use local serial ports to secure sensitive information.
- Cryptographically secured traffic management should be enabled with protocols such as SNMPv3.
- Security features should be enhanced on all devices periodically.

### Risks Due to Public Wireless Networks

Public wireless connections cannot be trusted for reliability and security, because they aim to provide network access to users freely. The major threats posed by these public networks are:

- Anyone can use the network, including the intruders.
- They act as a bridge between the user and the network, and hackers can access that bridge.
- High radio-frequency transmission allows intruders to snoop the signals.

If companies do not secure their networks from attacks due to public access, they may lose critical information when users connect to the public network. Users should also be trained to differentiate between the company's own assets and public resources. Public assets must be secured at the application layer of the network. Protocols, such as Transport Layer Security (TLS) and SSL, should be used in the application layer to accomplish this. Companies should connect to the network through a VPN, which ensures that unauthorized persons do not access the resources.

### Wired Equivalent Privacy (WEP)

The 802.11 MAC implementation specifies a protocol called Wired Equivalent Privacy (WEP). This is made to protect both the validation of data and the secrecy of data. WEP uses an RC4 cipher password for authentication.

There are a few disadvantages with WEP. First, it does not take the problem of managing the keys into consideration. As the number of user keys increases, the likelihood of someone inadvertently sharing the key with an outsider also increases. Also, WEP is vulnerable to password crackers.

## Wireless Network Security Tools

### WEPCrack

WEPCrack is a set of Perl scripts used to crack WEP keys. These scripts include the following:

- *WeakIVGen.pl*: This creates a file called IVfile.log that contains IVs (initialization vectors) meant to weaken each character of the WEP key.
- *prism-getIV.pl*: This script reads prismdump and Ethereal capture files, and looks for weak IVs in WEP traffic. When it finds them, it places them in IVfile.log along with the first encrypted output byte. It gets input from stdin or from a file specified at the command line.
- *WEPCrack.pl*: This script reads IVfile.log and uses the weak IVs with the encrypted output to determine the WEP key. It sometimes guesses incorrectly, so users should be sure to test its output.
- *Prism-decode.pl*: This reads prismdump and Ethereal capture files, and decodes 802.11 frames. It gets input from stdin or from a file specified at the command line.

### AirSnort

AirSnort uses known susceptibilities in the key scheduling algorithm of R4, which forms the foundation of the WEP standard. The software analyzes data sent over a WLAN in passive mode and generates encryption keys

**Figure 5-13** Wellenreiter can scan for
wireless networks, even those that do
not broadcast their SSIDs.

after approximately 100 MB of network packets have been detected. On a hectic network, gathering this much data may require only three or four hours. However, if traffic levels are low, it could easily take a few days. After all network packets have been analyzed, the WEP key can be obtained in a few milliseconds.

## Aircrack

Aircrack is a set of tools for detecting wireless networks. It includes an 802.11 sniffer and a WEP/WPA key cracker. Aircrack consists of the following tools:

- *Airodump*: 802.11 packet capture program
- *Aireplay*: 802.11 packet injection program
- *Aircrack*: Static WEP and WPA-PSK key cracker
- *Airdecap*: Decrypts WEP/WPA capture files

## AirSnarf

AirSnarf is a simple rogue wireless access point setup service. It was developed and released to uncover an inherent vulnerability of public 802.11b hotspots, stealing usernames and passwords by confusing users with DNS and HTTP redirects from an opposing AP.

## Wellenreiter

Wellenreiter is a wireless network discovery and auditing tool, shown in Figure 5-13. It is fairly easy to use because the NIC does not need to be configured, and it has a useful GUI.

Wellenreiter can discover networks, whether they broadcast their SSIDs or not, along with their WEP capabilities and the manufacturer name. DHCP and ARP traffic is automatically decoded and displayed to produce more information about the networks. An Ethereal/Tcpdump-compatible dump file and an application save file are automatically created. Using a supported GPS device and GPSd, the location of the discovered networks can be charted.

# Wireless Standards

Products that comply with any of these standards are considered to be Wi-Fi certified, and all support WEP and WPA security.

## IEEE 802.11a (Wi-Fi)

- *Data rate*: Up to 54 Mbps in the 5-GHz band
- *Modulation scheme*: Orthogonal frequency division multiplexing (OFDM)

Eight channels are available, which is not enough to avoid interference. It is superior to 802.11b in terms of maintaining large amounts of data in highly populated user setups, which is a comparatively smaller range than 802.11b. There is no interoperability with 802.11b.

## IEEE 802.11b (Wi-Fi)

- *Data rate*: Up to 11 Mbps in the 2.4-GHz band
- *Modulation scheme*: DSSS with CCK

There is no interoperability with 802.11a. It requires fewer access points than 802.11a to cover large areas and gives faster access to data at a range of 300 feet from the base station.

## IEEE 802.11g (Wi-Fi)

- *Data rate*: Up to 54 Mbps in the 2.4-GHz band
- *Modulation scheme*: OFDM above 20 Mbps, DSSS with CCK below 20 Mbps

This is compliant with 802.11b and has several security enhancements.

## IEEE 802.11n

The 802.11n standard uses new technology and tweaks existing technologies to give Wi-Fi more speed and range. It includes the following technologies:

- Multiple input, multiple output (MIMO)
- Channel bonding, which involves using two separate nonoverlapping channels at the same time to transmit data

# Techniques and Tools for Securing Wireless Communications

To protect a wireless network, first follow these basic steps:

- Use encryption. This is the most effective way to secure a wireless network from intruders. Most wireless routers, access points, and base stations have a built-in encryption mechanism.
- Use antivirus and antispyware software, and a firewall. On a wireless network, computers need the same protections as any other computer connected to the Internet. Be sure the firewall is always on and the antivirus and antispyware software is kept updated.
- Turn off SSID broadcasting. Wireless routers have an identifier broadcasting mechanism that sends out a signal to any device in the vicinity. There is no need to broadcast this information if everyone using the network already knows it. Hackers exploit SSID broadcasting to find vulnerable wireless networks.
- Change the SSID on the router from the default. Hackers often attempt to use default SSIDs to access networks.
- Change the router's default administrator password.

## Authentication

The following are the types of authentication mechanisms commonly used in a wireless network:

- Open system
- Shared key

- IEEE 802.1x
- WPA or WPA2 with preshared key

## Open System

This is not actually authentication because it involves discovering a wireless node using its wireless adapter hardware address. Hardware addresses for the network adapter are assigned at the time of its manufacture and are used to discover the source and destination address of wireless frames. It is very simple for a hacker to capture frames sent out on the wireless network that contain the hardware address of permitted wireless nodes and to use that information to join the network.

## Shared Key

In the authentication process, the wireless client shows that it has knowledge of the secret key, such as a WEP key, without sending that key. All wireless clients and the wireless AP use the same shared key in infrastructure mode. Likewise, all wireless clients in an ad hoc wireless network use the same shared key.

## IEEE 802.1x

The IEEE 802.1x standard identifies the authentication of a network node before it starts to exchange data with the network. No frame will be exchanged with the network if the authentication process fails. This standard was developed for wired Ethernet networks and later adapted for use by 802.11. IEEE 802.1x uses Extensible Authentication Protocol (EAP) and specific authentication methods to authenticate network nodes.

This provides stronger authentication than open system or shared key. It uses EAP-Transport Layer Security (TLS) and digital certificates for authentication. For wireless connections to use EAP-TLS authentication, there must be an authentication infrastructure containing an Active Directory domain, Remote Authentication Dial-In User Service (RADIUS) servers, and certification authorities (CAs) to issue certificates to the RADIUS servers and wireless clients. This authentication is suitable for large businesses and enterprise organizations, but is not practical for home or small business offices.

## WPA or WPA2 with Preshared Key

WPA and WPA2 use a preshared key authentication method. This key is used on the wireless AP and every wireless client. Every initial WPA or WPA2 encryption key is unique.

The WPA or WPA2 preshared key should be a random sequence of either keyboard characters (upper and lowercase letters, numbers, and punctuation) at least 20 characters long or hexadecimal digits (numbers 0–9 and letters A–F) at least 24 digits long. The more random the key is, the safer it is to use. Unlike the WEP key, the WPA or WPA2 preshared key cannot be determined by gathering a large amount of encrypted data. Therefore, the key does not need to be changed frequently.

# LDAP

The X.500 directory service model consists of a central repository of operating system information and management functionalities. The information database and querying protocol LDAP is based on this model. It works to combine the details of system services and application services to make them compatible with each other and to provide an easy way to configure data related to application programs, security, and user accounts on the local network.

The design of LDAP does not support a large number of user entries and user databases, but is a hierarchical database in the form of records with few entries. The directory structure of LDAP is similar to the file structure in Windows. Small, simple records are used to provide faster access. LDAP is not compatible with large databases such as Oracle, Sybase, DB/2 and SQL Server.

There are a few different LDAP servers, including the following:

- DS series LDAP directory (AIX), designed by IBM
- Innosoft's Distributed Directory Server for Linux
- Netscape Directory Server for Linux
- OpenLDAP server for Linux
- Sun Microsystems' Directory Services for Solaris
- SLAPD, designed by the University of Michigan

Novell's eDirectory and Lotus Domino use the LDAP protocol as an interface to communicate with the directories that work with LDAP. Microsoft's Active Directory supports the LDAP protocol as well.

Users of the LDAP protocol communicate with its directory server for authentication. A bind function is performed to validate the client. The permissions of the user and the type of authentication mechanism are chosen and passed to the server during the bind function. LDAP authorizes clients with an ACL (access control list).

LDAP has the following benefits:

- Has an application server to collect details such as personal data and contact details from the directory
- Answers client queries that are in its repository with the help of its search engine
- DNS servers store information in the LDAP record hierarchy
- Used as an interface gateway to exchange data between incompatible applications
- System services such as the RADIUS and Kerberos use the LDAP protocol to store location details in the LDAP database

## Communications

Communication through LDAP is either client-to-server or server-to-server. Client-to-server communication permits application programs to use LDAP commands for creating, retrieving, modifying, and deleting data. Server-to-server communication involves information location and retrieval, and a way of updating and changing information between multiple servers using LDAP's tree-structured repository.

## Architecture of LDAP

LDAP stores information in a hierarchical structured format. The data stored in LDAP is specific to each type of LDAP server. A certain set of LDAP servers is dedicated to provide login details, whereas another set of servers provides details of the host address that the DNS and DHCP servers use. The type of server used depends on the amount of data to be stored.

If there is a small amount of information, it is stored in a single structure called a Directory Information Tree (DIT). All LDAP information is stored in the subtrees of the DIT. Each node of the tree is called a DSE (Directory Service Entry), which contains the details of the records. The records consist of descriptions of the objects in the network like the details of users, devices, components, and privileges. Duplicate objects are renamed in the hierarchy. The root DSE consists of the details of the whole tree structure.

WLAN devices contain built-in LDAP client software, such as the Enterprise Wireless Gateways (EWGs). The interfacing of client and server software to authenticate users is critical in the architecture of wireless LANs. In LDAP used within wireless networks, RADIUS software is used to interface the servers and clients, and for user authentication by searching for user details in the LDAP directory structure. LDAP support enhances the security and scalability of wireless networks. In the same way, Kerberos is integrated into the LDAP-compatible Active Directory user repository to manage services in distributed platforms.

# Multifactor Authentication

With multifactor authentication, users are authenticated by taking into account more than one permission. The three fundamentals for the creation of multifactor authentication are:

- User accounts (usernames and passwords)
- Token, secure ID, or smart card
- Fingerprints, eye or hand scan, or keystroke dynamics

Two-factor authentication solutions manage both central and remote network devices, taking into account the integrity and security of the network. Still, the administrative overhead and complexity limit the authentication to two factors.

Installing security mechanisms in laptops of remote users, such as a smart card reader using digital signatures, increases the efficiency and cost of management. Biometric identification needs more time and is more expensive. SSO (single sign-on) is one method of user authentication that decreases administrative overhead, because the user does not need to remember a number of passwords to access different applications.

# Kerberos Authentication

Kerberos is a security method that provides verification and security to messages. Kerberos is the default authentication protocol for Windows 2000 Active Directory, Windows Server 2003 Active Directory, Windows 2000, and Windows XP clients. Kerberos provides both user verification and encryption keys to safeguard networks from all types of attacks on data in transfer, including disturbance, stoppage, alteration, and production. Kerberos applies a three-mode security approach: the client, the server, and the secure mediator (the key distribution center, or KDC).

Kerberos authentication has the following advantages:

- *Shared authentication*: The client can confirm the server's uniqueness, and servers can mutually confirm the uniqueness of each other. The client can authenticate its identity to the server.

- *Reliability management*: Kerberos trusts are mechanically designed and maintained between all of the areas in an Active Directory forest and are transferable in two ways. Reliability can also be designed between clusters, as well as between Windows Server 2003 Kerberos areas and other Kerberos executions.

- *Secure transit*: Messages are encrypted with a range of encryption keys to guarantee that no one can corrupt the client's ticket or other information in a Kerberos message. Kerberos also prohibits the original password, or any extension of it, from being transmitted across the network.

- *Prevention of retransmission of authentication packets*: Time stamps are used as a valuator to reduce the risk of someone attaining and recycling a Kerberos authentication packet. Windows 2000 original clock management requires each packet to be organized within a very short period of time of each other. Kerberos validation will not function if this rule is broken.

## Components of the Kerberos System

- *KDC (Key distribution center)*: The KDC is the network service that offers both TGTs and service tickets to users and computers on the network. The KDC administers the verification between a user and a server. The KDC offers two services: the Authentication Service (AS) and the Ticket-Granting Service (TGS). The AS issues TGTs for association to the TGS. The TGS then offers the user a service ticket for verification with the end network service. The AS sends back a TGT for the TGS, which can be reused until it expires.

- *TGT (Ticket-granting ticket)*: The AS grants the TGT to users initially when they validate with the KDC. After the user gets the TGT, he or she can provide it to the TGS to request a service ticket.

- *Service ticket*: The TGS grants a service ticket to a user in response to the user sending a TGT. After the user gets a service ticket, the user can offer this to a network service in order to validate with the service and start a session. The service ticket is encoded using a common key for the KDC. This guarantees that the end server is validated because only the server can decode the session.

- *Transfer ticket*: The transfer ticket is initially a TGT to the domain where the store is located and is arranged any time a user tries to link to an end server that is a member of a different domain. The AS and TGS functions are distinct within the KDC, allowing the user to use the TGT obtained from the AS to get service tickets from a TGS in other domains through the use of transfer tickets. The transfer ticket is encrypted using a key shared between two different areas, the initial domain and the target domain, that is exchanged as part of the establishment of transitive reliable relationships.

## Exchanges of a Kerberos Client

- *AS exchange*: The KDC uses the AS exchange to present a user with a session key for logging on and a TGT for service ticket requests. Once the user is authenticated, a TGT certified for the local domain is issued. The TGT has an original life span of 10 hours and may be extended over the user's session without the user needing to retype a password. The TGT is stored on the local machine in memory space that can be exhausted and used to request sessions with services all over the network.

- *TGS exchange*: The KDC uses the TGS exchange to distribute service session keys and service tickets. The user produces the TGT to the TGS portion of the KDC when attempting to gain access to a server service. The TGS on the KDC authenticates the user's TGT and creates a ticket and session key for both the client and the inaccessible server. This information, called the service ticket, is then stored locally on the client workstation. The TGS gets the client's TGT and accesses it using its own key. If the TGS agrees with the client's request, a service ticket is produced for both the client and the end server. The service ticket that is sent back is encoded using the master key common to the KDC and the objective server so only the target server can decode the service ticket. The client accesses its segments using the TGS session key derived prior to the AS reply. The client offers the server segment of the TGS response to the objective server in the client/server interchange.

- *Client/Server authentication exchange*: This exchange is used when presenting a service ticket to a target service on the network. After the client user has the client/server service ticket, a session can be set up with the server. The server can decode the information coming from the TGS using its self-distant goal key obtained from the KDC. The service ticket is then used to validate the client user and set up a service session between the server and client. After the ticket's life span is exhausted, the service ticket must be extended to use the service.

## WPA

WPA is a wireless security mechanism that uses a subset of IEEE 802.11i to act as a powerful, standards-based, and interoperable security technology.

WPA provides powerful data protection by utilizing encryption, strong access controls, and user authentication. It uses 128-bit encryption keys and dynamic session keys for wireless network privacy and enterprise security.

WPA uses TKIP, discussed later in this chapter, to address these weaknesses:

- *Replay attacks*: IVs cannot be utilized when they are not available
- *Forgery attacks*: ICV using 32-bit CRC is straightforward and can be changed
- *Key collision attacks*: IV collisions
- *Weak-key attacks*: RC4 stream cipher is susceptible to FMS attack tools such as AirSnort, WEPCrack, and dweputils

In addition, it uses 802.1x to resolve these weaknesses:

- Absence of key management
- Absence of support for authentication methods such as tokens, smart cards, certificates, biometrics, and one-time passwords
- Absense of user authorization and identification support
- Lack of significant authentication or authorization

There are two types of WPA: WPA-Personal and WPA-Enterprise. WPA-Personal uses a password to protect unauthorized network access, while WPA-Enterprise authenticates the user through a server.

### Features of WPA

- *WPA authentication*: WPA requires 802.1x authentication. It uses preshared keys for environments without a RADIUS infrastructure and uses Extensible Authentication Protocol (EAP) and RADIUS for environments with a RADIUS infrastructure.
- *WPA key management*: With WPA, it is necessary to rekey both unicast and global encryption keys. For unicast keys, Temporal Key Integrity Protocol (TKIP) changes the key for every frame. With a global key, WPA uses the wireless AP to announce the changed key to connected wireless clients.
- *Temporal key management*: TKIP uses an encryption algorithm that is stronger than the WEP algorithm.
- *Michael algorithm*: In 802.11 and WEP data, integrity is provided by a 32-bit integrity check value (ICV). In WPA, the Michael algorithm determines an 8-byte message integrity code (MIC) with the help of methods present in wireless devices. This MIC is located between the data portion of an IEEE 802.11 frame and the 4-byte ICV. The MIC gets encrypted with the frame data and the ICV.
- *AES support*: WPA supports Advanced Encryption Standard (AES) as a substitute for WEP encryption. This support is optional, depending on whether the vendor chooses to support it.
- *Supports a mixture of WPA and WEP wireless clients*: Most wireless APs maintain both WEP and WPA simultaneously, to help the gradual transition of WEP-based wireless networks to WPA.

WPA is shown in Figure 5-14.

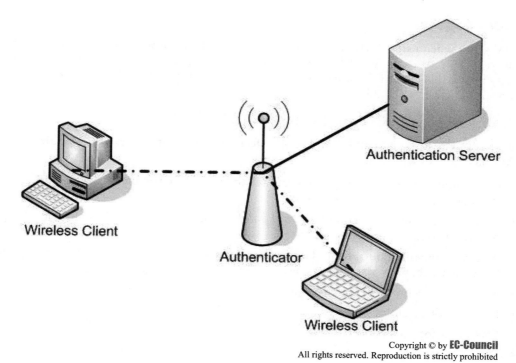

**Figure 5-14**   Most wireless hardware supports WPA.

## Temporal Key Integrity Protocol (TKIP)

TKIP has three main elements that increase encryption:

- Key integration function for individual packets
- Enhanced message integrity code (MIC) function, named Michael
- Improved IV, including sequencing guidelines

TKIP is a short-term fix for WEP, organized as a simple software/firmware upgrade. It contains a number of deliberate design weaknesses in order to maintain backward compatibility with existing hardware. TKIP detects all of the identified weaknesses linked with WEP.

The client initiates with two keys: a 128-bit encryption key and a 64-bit data integrity key acquired steadily during the 802.1x compromise. The encryption key is known as the temporal key (TK), while the integrity key is known as the message integrity code (MIC) key. First, the dispatcher's MAC address is XORed with the TK to generate the Phase 1 key (also known as the intermediary key). The Phase 1 key is then combined with a series number to create the Phase 2, per-packet key. The yield of Phase 2 is passed to the WEP engine as a typical 128-bit WEP key (IV + shared secret). The remaining process occurs as an ordinary WEP transaction. The difference is that there are no more clients using the identical WEP key (because of Phase 1) and there is no longer any association between the IV individual packet key mixing.

Compromise key attacks are overcome because the IV can no longer be associated to the per-packet key. The difficulty with the original WEP design was that the IV was appended to the secret key and just plugged into RC4. Under TKIP, Phase 1 guarantees that every client has a different intermediate key. Then, Phase 2 combines the key with a series number before it is plugged into RC4. TKIP's employment of a per-packet key solves WEP's inappropriate RC4 implementation.

### Michael: TKIP's MIC Function

The MIC function, or Michael, uses a one-direction hash function. Since it is not linear, it is difficult for an attacker to alter the packet in transfer. Michael requires the MIC key, source address, destination address, and plaintext. By integrating the source and destination addresses, MAC integrity can be established. Michael output is 8 bytes long and is attached to the data field.

### Larger IV Space

The IV space when using TKIP increases from 24 to 48 bits. At 54 Mbps, this means that it would take over 1,000 years to repeat an IV. TKIP requires that IVs increment from 0 and drop out of sequence packets. In security terms, this larger IV space (sequence number) means that IV collisions and their associated attacks are no longer realistically possible.

## Counter-Mode/CBC-MAC Protocol (CCMP)

Like TKIP, CCMP resolves all known WEP defects, but without the restraints of already deployed hardware. CCMP has the following features:

- Uses a single key to provide privacy and reliability, reduce key management load, and lessen the time spent generating AES key schedules
- Provides reliability protection for the plaintext frame header, as well as integrity and privacy of the packet payload
- Allows recompilation to reduce latency; since frames can be lost, the receiver may perform recompilation for a packet that never reaches its destination; however, the sender's attempts are rarely rejected
- Maintains pipelining to increase output
- Has a small execution size
- Small cost for each packet
- Does not contain patented methods

CCMP has many features in common with TKIP, but it is free of the restrictions caused by legacy hardware. As with TKIP, CCMP uses a 48-bit IV, so key management can be restricted to the beginning of an association and ignored for its life span. CCMP uses this 48-bit IV as a series number to provide replay recognition, just like TKIP.

However, AES has considerable differences from the RC4 encryption algorithm used by WEP and TKIP. AES has no need for per-packet keys, so CCMP has no per-packet key derivation function. CCMP uses the same AES key (and associated AES key schedule) to offer privacy and reliability protection for all packets in an association. CCMP uses an eight-octet MIC, which is considerably stronger than Michael.

## Wireless Transport Layer Security (WTLS)

WTLS is similar to Secure Socket Layer (SSL) protocol, but developed for the wireless environment. It provides security and reliability for data transmission in client/server communications. For secure wireless transactions and encrypted connections, the client and the server must be authenticated.

SSL provides security over the Internet, but WTLS is specific to wireless applications using WAP. WTLS is secure over TLS and SSL with respect to the restrictions present in the wireless application environment.

The major disadvantage is that WTLS allows weak encryption algorithms. With some WAP clients, users can even disable WTLS encryption entirely. The available options restrict the security of a WAP application.

## Extensible Authentication Protocol (EAP) Methods

### EAP-TLS

EAP-TLS is frequently used in WLANs. EAP-TLS authentication is based on X.509 certificates. In WLAN usage, the STA (station) must have a certificate that the AS (authentication server) can validate. Similarly, the AS will present a certificate to the STA and the STA has to validate it. In other words, there is mutual authentication between the AS and STA. This is achieved by having both certificates issued by one, preferably independent and secure, CA (certification authority); each party has the CA's certificate and CRL (certificate revocation list) to be able to validate the certificates. After the authentication, a shared session secret between the AS and the STA is created and exchanged. The AS provides this to the authenticator system through a secure link, and the authenticator system and the STA can use it to initialize their per-packet, authenticated, secure, encrypted communication. Because of this mutual authentication, EAP-TLS is resistant to man-in-the-middle attacks. If an attacker attempts to intercept the exchange, he or she will not succeed.

The complexity of a PKI is required by EAP-TLS to support STA authentication. This may be possible in large corporate deployments, but it may be unreasonable for small and medium businesses. A strong password authentication method using user IDs and passwords is more feasible for many public deployments.

EAP-TLS support is available in Microsoft XP workstations and as part of the WLAN software for other operating systems. To reduce the complexity and expenses of deploying the user certificates required to support EAP-TLS, two methods have been introduced that use a server-side certificate to allow server authentication and creation of an EAP-TLS tunnel that transmits other authentication methods over the tunnel. The two methods that have been proposed are PEAP (Protected EAP) and EAP-TTLS (Tunneled TLS).

## PEAP

Protected EAP (PEAP) extends the TLS challenge to carry an EAP exchange. After the primary TLS exchange is completed, authenticating the server to the user, any other EAP method can be used to authenticate the user to the server. Two EAP exchanges occur: the first sets up TLS, and the second is for protection purposes.

Characteristics of PEAP include:

- Providing certificate-based AS authentication by using standard TLS methodology
- Authenticating the STA's AS to the STA
- STA authentication using any EAP type within EAP-TLS tunnel
- STA identity hiding by using a generic identity in outer EAP and the real identity within TLS
- Fast reconnection using TLS session resume

PEAP does not ignore all of the PKI (public key infrastructure) complexity of TLS. The AS must have certificates and the STA must be configured with the root certificate of the AS to verify the AS name within the AS certificate. This prevents a man-in-the-middle attack from rogue APs. STAs must also use some form of certificate verification to ensure that the AS certificate has not been revoked. For example, CRLs and OCSP are both protocols for checking certificate validity.

Internal EAP success and failure messages are within the TLS tunnel. EAP failure is presented in clear text if outer EAP-TLS fails. This is different from TTLS, where all EAP success and failure messages are presented clearly.

## EAP-TTLS

EAP-TTLS provides a secure channel standard TLS methodology, which in turn provides certificate-based authentication.

It authenticates the AP's AS to the STA, unlike TLS, which only authenticates the STA's AS to the STA. STA authentication uses standard PPP methods as well as any EAP type within PPP.

## EAP-SRP

EAP-SRP is a strong password alternative method to TLS. SRP has some intellectual property issues compared to other methods, but is very resistant to attacks. Because it only uses user IDs and passwords, it is simple to deploy in many organizations. As with TLS or TTLS, there is no explicit authentication of the AS by the STA. SRP only provides mutual authentication implicitly. This may limit SRP's functionality in situations where the AS is resistant to user database espionage, or where loss of the user database can be easily corrected.

## Advanced Encryption Standard (AES)

The Advanced Encryption Standard (AES) is presently the preferred information protection encryption algorithm. It is unclassified and used by the National Institute of Standards and Technology (NIST) of the United States to shield federal information and communications. AES uses a Rijndael algorithm that implements symmetric key cryptography as a block cipher, with a block size of 128 bits and key sizes of 128, 192, and 256 bits.

The AES algorithm has the following features:

- Security features, including resistance of the algorithm to cryptanalysis, strong mathematical basis, random algorithm output, and relative security as compared to others
- Cost effectiveness must be evaluated for licensing requirements, computational speed, efficiency on different platforms, and memory requirements
- Implementation must be flexible and supports configured hardware and software

Rijndael is a recursive block cipher that applies transformation cycles on the initial input block with the cipher keys to generate a new output. It applies round operations on the input and each round has a round key of

128 bits. This generated output will act as an input for the next round. Performing inverse functions of the round operations on the output will decrypt it.

The Rijndael algorithm supports 10, 12, or 14 rounds depending on the basis of the key sizes. Its round function consists of four layers. The first layer applies an eight-by-eight S-box to each byte. The second and third layers provide linear mixing to the first layer, in which the rows of the array are shifted and the columns are mixed. The fourth layer XORs the subkey bytes into each byte of the array without any column mixing.

## Data Encryption Standard (DES)

Data Encryption Standard (DES) is the most popular standard for data encryption. It was developed by IBM and officially recognized by the U.S. government in 1977. DES uses a symmetric cryptosystem to encrypt and decrypt messages. Both the sender and the receiver must share the same secret key. DES translates the plaintext into a sequence of bits (0s and 1s) in blocks of 64 bits each, padded with trailing 0s when necessary.

In DES, this encoded bit pattern is given as input into the algorithm and corresponding ciphertext, and is given as output and returned by the algorithm. Feistel ciphers are applied to plaintext to form a ciphertext by going through 16 rounds. The encrypted text is split into two halves. The round function $f$ is applied to one half using a subkey, and the output of the function is XORed with the other half. Then the two halves are swapped. The same pattern is applied to each round. In the last round, swapping is not done.

### *Triple DES*

Triple DES acquires key lengths of 192 bits and segments them into three subkeys. The segmented parts are padded with other bits to frame them to 64 bits. It repeats the same pattern as that of simple DES three times. The data is encrypted with the first key, decrypted with the second key, and finally reencrypted with the third key. It is slower than standard DES, but is also more secure.

## RSA Encryption

RSA does not involve complicated cryptoalgorithms. It is very simple, easy to use, and based on the principles of modulo arithmetic.

It is represented by the function $z$ modulo $n$, or $z$ mod $n$. Its output is the remainder when $z$ is divided by $n$. Modulo arithmetic is also called clock arithmetic. This method can be applied to a large number of integers with absolute accuracy.

## WAP (Wireless Application Protocol)

Wireless Application Protocol (WAP), shown in Figure 5-15, is an important standard for wireless devices, providing a link between the mobile network and the Internet. WAP describes the Wireless Application

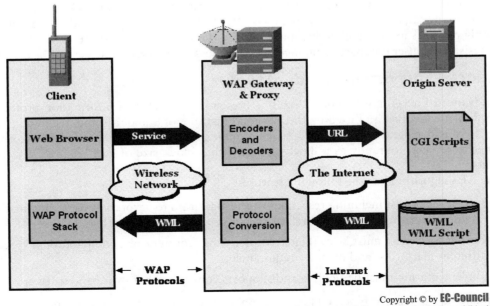

**Figure 5-15**    WAP is the standard markup language for mobile devices.

Environment (WAE), which allows operators, manufacturers, and developers to create new services and applications. The WAP protocol stack is created to reduce the required bandwidth and increase the number of wireless network types that can deliver WAP content.

WAP uses Wireless Markup Language (WML), based on the Extensible Markup Language (XML). It is used to define the content and user interface for narrow-band devices like cellular phones. In addition to XML, WAP uses Internet standards like User Datagram Protocol (UDP) and Internet Protocol (IP).

WML is made up of a number of cards, with each card containing a screen of information. The collection of cards is known as a deck; this deck is the same as an HTML page. WML is case sensitive, and all tabs and attributes are always in lowercase.

### WAP Micro Browser

A WAP micro browser is a Web browser designed for small wireless devices. Micro browsers are optimized to show Internet content on small screens of handheld devices and to accommodate lower memory capacity and bandwidth.

The micro browser interprets a version of JavaScript known as WMLScript. With the help of WMLScript, users can access user-agent facilities, check user input, and execute user-agent software.

# Developing a Wireless Security Policy

The creation of a wireless security policy involves the following steps:

- Identifying the resources that are to be protected
- Determining the threats from which the system should be protected
- Determining the probability of these threats
- Executing defensive measures
- Assessing vulnerabilities and enhancing security

In some cases, it costs more to employ security policies than to recover from the attacks. These policies are to be designed so that they are specific to the organization's security requirements.

## Identifying the Resources to Be Protected

Identifying assets and assessing the risks associated with each of them is the first step. This can assist in identifying the threats that may occur on an entire group of similar resources. After identifying the assets, the administration team recognizes the threats that might attack these resources. The administration team audits the threats to determine the potential damages.

## Determining the Probability of Threats

Determining the occurrence of threats helps the company focus on benefits rather than recovery from losses. The damage from outsiders is usually less compared to the loss caused by staff members and former staff members. Threats should be ranked depending on the probability of occurrence so as to plan for measures to secure assets. By prioritizing the risks, solutions can be implemented to economically solve security issues.

## Executing Defensive Measures

The assessment of risk determines the security of the entire network. If decisions are not taken in view of security goals, the security of the network will likely fail.

## Goals and Characteristics

### Services at Hand Versus Security

Services granted to users are not always free of risks. With some services, the risk for providing the service is greater than its benefit. In these cases, the network administrator must remove these services rather than providing costly security to them.

### Ease of Use Versus Security

Fewer passwords make systems easy to use, but they also make them less secure. A balance must be reached between ease of use and security.

### Price to Secure Versus Threat of Loss

Tighter security costs more money, but it also means lower risk. Again, the proper balance must be determined.

### Security Policy

The security policy is a set of rules issued by the administration to enhance the security of services provided. It contains permissions regarding who is authorized to access specific resources. It details the risks due to misuse of the assets and the damage that can occur to the assets due to unauthorized access.

### The Intention of Applying Security Policies

The purpose of a security policy is to notify the staff, managers, and users about their responsibility to protect technical and information resources. It explains the requirements and the methods used to secure the assets, including configuring and auditing computers to be compatible with the policy. It includes an acceptable use policy (AUP), which mentions the rights and responsibilities regarding the security of the systems. The AUP also mentions the types of traffic that can be permitted into the network as clearly as possible.

## Auditing WLAN Security Policy

### Review

Security policies should be regularly reviewed. Modifications of the policy should be relayed to the employees of the organization. All staff should be trained on any new methodologies as soon as possible.

### Assess

The processes of the organization need to be assessed. Some companies employ a third-party assessment company to assess their security strengths and weaknesses. This helps to both identify and prevent threats. Modifications that are suggested are to be recorded and displayed to all employees of the company. The security policy document should be updated to reflect any changes.

### Awareness Programs

Employees must to be trained in the security policies. Ignorance of security policies can result in damages to the company's assets by its staff. It is important to educate employees on both the necessity of the policies and the potential loss when they are violated. The staff should acknowledge the security policies with their signatures on a document listing the security rules. Employees tend to view security as a hindrance to working efficiently, so they must be trained on how the policies actually increase efficiency.

## RADIUS

The RADIUS protocol is an organized protocol used to access the network. The protocol is easy to use and efficient, despite some problems with security and data transfer.

Accessing the network using RADIUS involves the following steps:

- Enter username and password
- User information is transferred through NAS (Network Access Server) to the RADIUS server
- The RADIUS server compares these details with the database

In a wireless LAN, the AP acts as the NAS. RADIUS stores data in its internal database or an external database. It uses a user-based authentication mechanism. Hardware authentication mechanisms are carried out through MAC addresses and shared keys, like WEP keys. Switching from hardware to user-based authentication ensures scalability and security of WLANs. If RADIUS is implemented in a wired network, it is easy to use it in a wireless network in the same organization.

Benefits of using RADIUS include the following:

- Authentication does not rely on hardware
- Economical
- Decreases operating costs for the administrators when data are changed

- Accounting, assessment, and reporting are supported features of RADIUS that also warn regarding unauthorized access of the network
- Can be used with a VPN in a wireless network

The distinction between the wireless VPN implementation of RADIUS and the user-based implementation is the type of NAS devices used and the authenticating protocol. The RADIUS server deals with the type of supporting protocol. The security mechanism should be built to combat attacks.

## Performance

Performance of RADIUS relies on selection of the server and the server's attributes. These attributes include accounting, scalability, and clustering and failover support.

*Accounting* Statistics of the connection, such as the connection speed, time, usage, data transfer rate, and amount of data transferred in a specified time, are stored in the log files of the system and the database used by the RADIUS protocol. The users that are connected to the network and the RAS (Remote Access Servers) can also be viewed. These details are fed to the software that manages bills and charges the users for simultaneous logins. The central service provider manages the accounting details of the entire organization.

*Scalability* The RADIUS server is compatible with Windows, Linux, and UNIX operating systems. Scalability, available features, and future upgrade support increase the cost of the RADIUS server. The RADIUS server is configured with the administrative tool software. The more precise the server features, the more efficiently it works with the specific needs of the corporate network. It is recommended to configure reasonably priced RADIUS servers for better scalability to execute key distribution, proxy authentication, and other wireless authentication functions within the company's network. WLANs make use of these scalable RADIUS servers to execute the 802.1x/EAP in different designs.

*Clustering and Failover Support* Clustering is when a number of computers with different operating systems and processing speeds execute the same applications. In such cases, the computers need to install operating systems with additional features to support RADIUS, which may need licenses, privileges, and regular upgrading. Redundancy and failover are the primary advantages of clustering. When a number of computers work on the central database, the loss of data can be prevented and CPU power and speed can be utilized efficiently.

- *EAP support*: The RADIUS server should be compatible with an organization's existing server configuration. Wireless devices should be selected that are compatible with the EAP types and the wired network devices that use the RADIUS server.

- *Legacy authentication protocol support*: RADIUS should be implemented by selecting NAS protocols and the protocols that support them. The current RADIUS server version supports MS-CHAP, MS-CHAPv2, and various EAPs and other authenticating protocols. If the older versions of authentication protocols are compatible with the recent versions, they can be combined to form an efficient and cost-effective security solution, which is commonly used in VPN security and 802.1x/EAP-based security solutions.

- *Mutual authentication support*: Man-in-the-middle attacks are possible with one-way authentication. Mutual authentication eliminates this risk by authenticating the RADIUS server and the client. The client initially passes its identification to the server, which responds with its identification so that both the server and the client are assured of mutual reliability. The same happens with the AP and the server.

## Configuration

*Central Authenticity and Security* The RADIUS server is configured on a central network or network hub to which individual networks connect for authentication. It is costly to configure the RADIUS server on every network individually. The central RADIUS server handles the authentication and security of these networks. It manages the querying of users, maintains user account details, and stores accounting information for billing at the central site. The reliability of the network depends on the security provided to the central site. In a distributed network environment with a central RADIUS server, the load is distributed and results in increased performance with less bandwidth usage.

*Mixture of Architectures* Networks that use RADIUS may not be compatible with other network types. If certain networks are not reliably connected to the central site on which the RADIUS server is configured, the RADIUS server must be installed separately. 802.1x has the advantage of being flexible in distributed environments.

*Distributed Sites* Distributed site security using central authentication consists of WLAN APs in every individual network to validate its users, whose database is in the central site or operating hub of the distributed network. RADIUS servers manage the APs, WLAN, and remote access of the network. A RADIUS server authenticates the local users of the network, establishes secure network connectivity to the users, and stores accounting information.

Bandwidth and availability of RADIUS in the central site is extremely important. It is not necessary to have RADIUS servers at every location.

Network connectivity for users depends on the availability of connecting between the distributed network and the central hub. If the link is down, a connection cannot be established. Rekeying is necessary for users who disconnect from the network when it is down, which ensures security of connectivity. The RADIUS server's duty is to initially authenticate the users and then periodically calculate the cryptographic keys for better security. Large numbers of WLANs can cause bottlenecks and congestion in the network, which can be eliminated by configuring the RADIUS servers in WLANs with large numbers of users. This situation usually occurs in reliable and fast network links and in a distributed environment where the user database is stored in a central repository accessible by the distributed network. Here, WLAN users are validated with tokens.

*Distributed Autonomous Sites* In distributed autonomous networks, the database is present on the individual networks, so user information is not stored in a central database. One or more RADIUS servers are configured in the autonomous network to handle the WLAN and remote access. In this situation, there is no need for a central RADIUS server. The RADIUS servers perform user validation in the current network by setting WLAN connections and storing accounting information. As the WLAN users increase, the number of RADIUS servers that handle the overhead can be increased to increase performance and security. The autonomy provided to the network makes it easy to deploy the databases that use LDAP, but not reliable for databases such as SQL that cannot be replaced easily.

*Single-Site Deployments* In a single-site network deployment, the users of the WLAN are at the same site where a central database is maintained to validate the users. Multiple RADIUS servers are employed to locate user details, manage the validation of users, secure connection establishment, and manage remote access. Users of the WLAN can be validated with the available server databases. In addition to RADIUS, APs increase the scalability of the network and make it simple to authenticate users with the back-end database. If the number of WLAN users increases, it is recommended to use a distributed site deployment.

## Wireless Auditing

Wireless auditing is the process of simulating attacks on a network to determine its strengths and weaknesses. This involves using the hardware, software, and mindset of an attacker.

### Hardware

A laptop is set up with a wireless network card, a high-gain antenna, and a vehicle. There is no need for a high-speed laptop or a special antenna. A low-priced and efficient antenna can be fashioned from a satellite television receiver or empty Pringles cans, like the one seen in Figure 5-16.

### Software

Free, easy-to-use, cross-platform software programs are used to collect network names from beacons and probes. Full protocol analyzers such as Ethereal and Mognet, shown in Figure 5-17, monitor and capture traffic in real time, including logins and passwords sent in clear text.

NetStumbler can communicate with a GPS receiver to record the latitude and longitude of detected networks. These coordinates are uploaded to a central database in order to generate street maps, like the one shown in Figure 5-18.

### Mind-Set

Serious attackers can perform network damage, blackmail, and corporate espionage. Other attackers choose their targets based on a desire for profit or revenge. Security means reducing risk, but typically not eliminating it. Elimination is not possible in most cases.

## Baselining

Baselining is a process in which the average load on a network is measured over a set time period, perhaps hours or days. These data are used as a measure against which irregular network traffic may be compared.

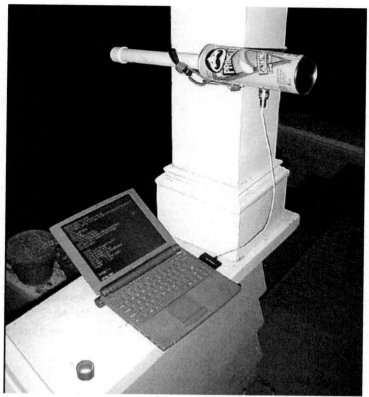

*Source:* http://www.node99.org/projects/waudit/waudit.pdf. Accessed 2004.

**Figure 5-16** A Pringles can makes a decent antenna.

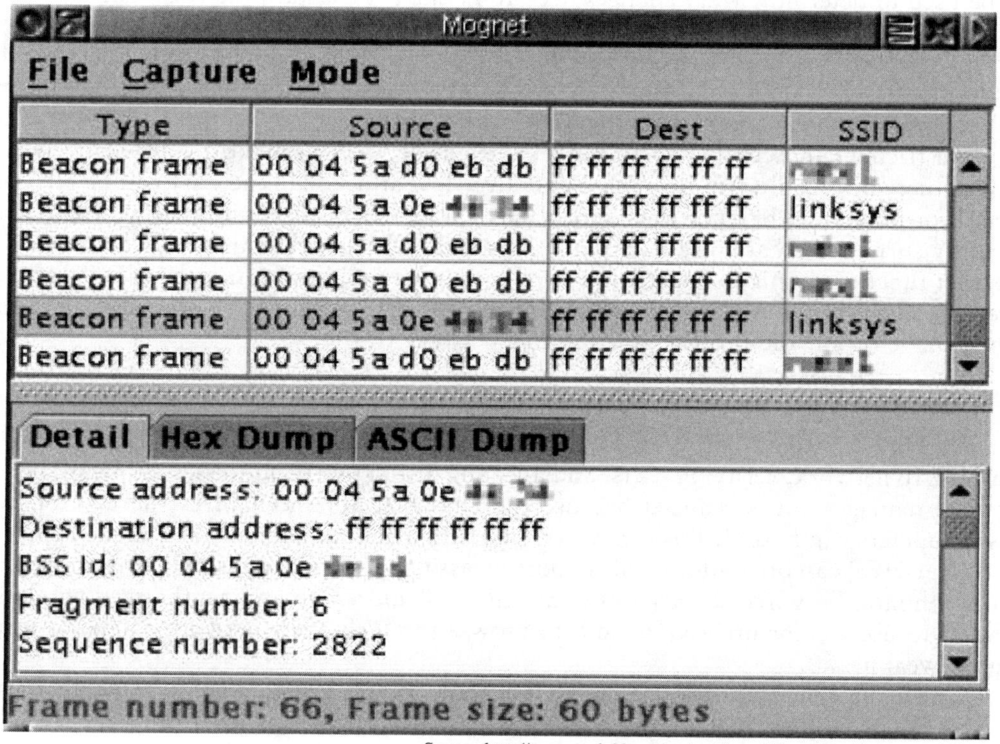

Mognet
File
Capture
Mode
Type
Source
Dest
SSID
Beacon frame
00 04 5a d0 eb db
ff ff ff ff ff ff
Beacon frame
00 04 5a 0e
ff ff ff ff ff ff
linksys
Beacon frame
00 04 5a d0 eb db
ff ff ff ff ff ff
Beacon frame
00 04 5a d0 eb db
ff ff ff ff ff ff
Beacon frame
00 04 5a 0e
ff ff ff ff ff ff
linksys
Beacon frame
00 04 5a d0 eb db
ff ff ff ff ff ff
Detail
Hex Dump
ASCII Dump
Source address: 00 04 5a 0e
Destination address: ff ff ff ff ff ff
BSS Id: 00 04 5a 0e
Fragment number: 6
Sequence number: 2822
Frame number: 66, Frame size: 60 bytes

*Source:* http://www.node99.org/projects/waudit/waudit.pdf. Accessed 2004.

**Figure 5-17** Mognet monitors and captures traffic in real time.

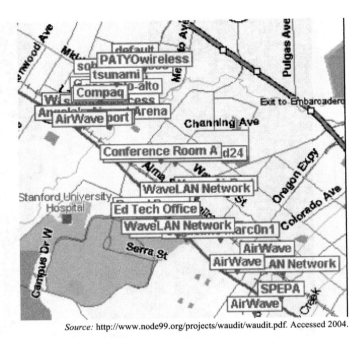

*Source:* http://www.node99.org/projects/waudit/waudit.pdf. Accessed 2004.

**Figure 5-18**  NetStumbler can generate street maps of detected access points.

Baselining can indicate whether network functionality is normal. Traffic extent and types present on the network over a range of time and at specific times of the day, or during definite days of the week, using a calculated load on the network infrastructure assets are used to describe data functionality as normal. Preferably, baselining is performed both before adding wireless network segments and after. This provides data that can be used to evaluate the impact of the WLAN on the network as a whole. The baseline suggestion information can be used to determine what changes need to be made to sustain the latest users and latest applications for the wireless network. A new baseline can be documented after supplementary users are added, and evaluated with the original baseline consequences to compute how much supplementary network bandwidth the extra load has used. An evaluation of the suggested baseline versus the present network performance can be used to help recognize problem areas within the wireless network.

The restricted bandwidth and half-duplex settings of WLANs make it comparatively easy for an attacker to inundate network bandwidth through a data overflow attack. This activity can be alleviated using minimum, average, or maximum baseline data verges and setting alarm verges in the IDS. If an attacker's activities significantly surpass the baseline, alarms are activated and security managers are informed. Abnormality-based detection functionality is frequently found in baselining tools and can react to DoS attacks that may go undetected. Baselines for DoS attack scrutiny allow for the improvement of more susceptible measures to be used in premature detection and reaction to abnormal network traffic.

## DHCP Services

Dynamic Host Configuration Protocol (DHCP) provides an arrangement for transferring information to hosts on a TCP/IP network, verifying users, and allotting distinctive IP addresses to inward network access requests. Network management is reduced because the DHCP server mechanizes the task of tracking IP addresses. New computers can be added to a network without having to manually assign each a unique IP address. With WLANs, DHCP can offer additional support by assigning IP addresses only to approved network users.

It is common for wireless networks to assign an IP address to an unauthorized wireless client. This permits a hacker to use a company's bandwidth to browse the Web, view network assets, or inspect the network for security weaknesses.

RFC 3118 appends authentication to DHCP and permits a client to confirm whether a specific DHCP server can be relied on and whether a request for DHCP information originates from a client that is certified to use the network. This mutual authentication in DHCP presents the additional security advantage of helping to protect DHCP clients and servers from DoS attacks and unauthorized access. RFC 3118 describes a method that can

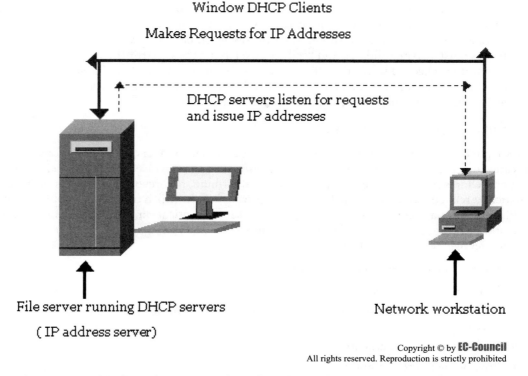

Window DHCP Clients

Makes Requests for IP Addresses

DHCP servers listen for requests
and issue IP addresses

File server running DHCP servers

( IP address server)

Network workstation

**Figure 5-19**   This shows how Network workstation and servers work together.

present both individual certification and message confirmation. This helps a DHCP client verify the uniqueness of the DHCP server it chooses in an unsecured network environment. This operation is very helpful for both a standard company Ethernet network and an Internet service provider (ISP).

## Client and Server

DHCP allows a client to easily join a network; thus, there are risks of DoS attacks, hijacking, and theft of services. DHCP denies bad and malevolent DHCP clients and servers, removing their ability to carry out DoS attacks or gain unauthorized access to the network. DHCP verification and allocation of fixed IPs can help reduce the risk of these types of attacks. Windows 2000 and XP clients mechanically restore their DHCP lease when their data-link layer link is lost and consequently reestablished. If a hacker steals the data-link connection of a legitimate user, the user is not able to reach the home network. The DSSS path in a wireless network can be blocked, causing a certified user to travel to a channel with less interference. By administering a malicious software AP on a laptop computer, along with DHCP server software, an attacker can block APs in close proximity, causing certified users to travel to the hacker's network.

After certified clients travel and lease an IP address from the malicious DHCP server, these clients can then be simply attacked using intrusion software in a peer-to-peer fashion through the AP. DoS attacks or theft can occur at layers 2 and 3 of the OSI model. Espionage of services can result from an attacker gaining access to an open network without approval. In many cases this will lead to gaining the use of open network resources. This type of access can also bring about illegal access to susceptible information, including a company's confidential matters and applications, or the ability to redesign segments of the network to permit further access.

Figure 5-19 shows the DHCP client and server model.

## Mobile Security Through Certificates

Third parties provide certificates for data security on mobile devices. Every certificate must include the entity's name and the public key. The digital signature on the certificate signs the public key. This certificate must be verified through a published SHA-1 or MD5 hash algorithm. The simplest architecture contains two certificates. One certificate has the public key of the entity to communicate, and the other certificate contains the public key of the entity that certifies the first certificate.

There are two types of certificates: root and chained. The owners of commercial entities recognized as trustworthy issue root certificates. The root certificate's originator is called a certificate authority (CA). Chained or intermediate certificates are the subordinate or low-level, certificates of the same trustworthy entities. These certificates must also be validated and verified by verifying the signature on data presented by an end entity (EE). The signature is checked to confirm that it actually belongs to that EE and is signed by the EE's CA.

Certificates have multiple formats, such as X.509 certificates, Pretty Good Privacy (PGP) certificates, and Simple Distributed Security Infrastructure (SDSI) certificates.

### Public Key Infrastructure (PKI)

A PKI (public key infrastructure) is a set of technologies that conducts communications by appending digital certificates to a message between two parties. The infrastructure involves the hardware, software, people, policies, and procedures needed to create, manage, store, distribute, and revoke certificates. It makes use of two mathematically related keys; the public key and the private key, in which one key cannot be derived from the other.

PKI supports a security architecture granting user authentication, data confidentiality, message authentication and integrity, and nonrepudiation. It involves both encryption and decryption.

An effective PKI must meet the following standards:

- Provides privacy between two parties exchanging data
- Ensures authentication to valid users
- Provides nonrepudiation, ensuring the presence of electronic events like signed contracts and wire transfers
- Provides access to authenticated users at all times
- Provides network scalability
- Provides security to private and public networks

# Troubleshooting Wireless Networks

The following are some steps for troubleshooting wireless networks:

1. *Eliminate user errors*: Ask users what they were doing when the problem first occurred. Often, user errors such as configuration changes or attempts to access unavailable resources are reported as network errors.
2. *Verify network connections*: Verify all the physical components on the affected computer, including interfaces, cables, antennae, and PC cards.
3. *Verify the status of network interfaces and access points*: If devices are properly connected and working, use any diagnostic information available to confirm that all the necessary pieces and parts are working properly. Most wireless interfaces and access points use colored LEDs for normal operation and to communicate problems. Also use access point tools and operating system networking tools.
4. *Restart the computer*: When all else fails, restart the computer and the server.

### Multipath

Changes to the physical environment can introduce conflicting signals. Try reconnecting.

### Hidden Node

This problem takes place when two or more users are attached to the same access point but are placed too far apart to see each other's transmission signal. Concurrent transmissions to the access point result in collisions.

# Developing a Wireless Network Security Checklist

A wireless network security checklist should contain at least the following items:

- Confirm that all ports not in use are closed.
- Regularly change SSIDs.
- Make sure that an authentication standard is developed and gets implemented.

- Make use of strong encryption for security purposes, such as SHA-1.
- Start the encryption at the user side and end it at the server behind the firewall, and outside the demilitarized zone (DMZ).
- Access confidential networks through VPNs and use two-factor authentication.
- Increase application security using an enterprise application system or encryption techniques.
- Do not allocate for ad hoc or peer-to-peer WLANs.
- Make use of the 802.11i IEEE security standard:
  - Apply access control for each user so that only a particular user can access the data.
  - Apply strong authentication methods such as tokens, smart cards, and certificates.
  - Apply strong encryption.

# Chapter Summary

- Wireless networking is quickly replacing traditional wired networking as the norm, both in the home and in the workplace, so wireless network security has become a hot topic.
- Access points are either hardware devices or software used to connect wireless users to a wired network.
- MExE allows for the secure download of applications for mobile computing and e-commerce purposes.
- Time division multiple access (TDMA) is a technology in which digital wireless transmission permits multiple users to use a single radio-frequency channel without interference, by assigning unique time slots to each user within the channel.
- Bluetooth links devices and creates point-to-point or multipoint WPANs (wireless personal area networks).
- Attackers use wardriving and warchalking to find unsecured wireless networks.
- Most of the same types of attacks that plague wired networks apply to wireless networks, and wireless networks have their own vulnerabilities because of the nature of wireless communications.
- WPA is a wireless security mechanism that uses a subset of IEEE 802.11i to act as a powerful, standards-based, and interoperable security technology.
- Wireless auditing is the process of simulating attacks on a network to determine its strengths and weaknesses.

# Review Questions

1. What is a wireless network?

   _____

   _____

   _____

   _____

2. List the types of wireless networks.

   _____

   _____

   _____

   _____

3. What is a peer-to-peer network?

_____

_____

_____

_____

4. What is the function of multiple access points?

_____

_____

_____

_____

5. How does a LAN-to-LAN wireless network work?

_____

_____

_____

_____

6. What are the advantages and disadvantages of a WLAN?

_____

_____

_____

_____

7. What are the components of a wireless network?

_____

_____

_____

_____

8. What is MExE?

_____

_____

_____

_____

9. What is TDMA?

_____

_____

_____

_____

10. What is CDMA?

_____

_____

_____

_____

11. What is RADIUS?

_____

_____

_____

_____

12. What is an SSID?

_____

_____

_____

_____

13. How do you detect rogue access points?

_____

_____

_____

_____

14. What is wardriving?

_____

_____

_____

_____

15. What are some wireless attacks?

_____

_____

_____

_____

16. What is social engineering?

_____

_____

_____

_____

17. What is WPA?

_____

_____

_____

_____

18. What is TKIP?

_____

_____

_____

_____

19. What is baselining?

_____

_____

_____

_____

20. What is PKI?

_____

_____

_____

_____

# Hands-On Projects

1. Read about wireless network security.

   ■ Navigate to Chapter 5 of the Student Resource Center.
   ■ Open Wireless Network Security.pdf and read the content.

2. Read a guide on setting up wireless networking.

   ■ Navigate to Chapter 5 of the Student Resource Center.
   ■ Open Set Up a Wireless LAN and read the content.

3. Read about high-speed wireless LAN options.

   ■ Navigate to Chapter 5 of the Student Resource Center.
   ■ Open High-Speed Wireless LAN Options.pdf and read the content.

4. Read about WLAN security issues.

   ■ Navigate to Chapter 5 of the Student Resource Center.
   ■ Open Wireless lan security issues.pdf and read the content.

5. Read about wireless network policy.

   ■ Navigate to Chapter 5 of the Student Resource Center.
   ■ Open Wireless Network Policy.pdf and read the content.

# Index